HAUNTED PUBS OF THE SOUTH WEST

HAUNTED PUBS OF THE SOUTH WEST

IAN ADDICOAT

AMBERLEY

First published 2009

Amberley Publishing
Cirencester Road, Chalford,
Stroud, Gloucestershire, GL6 8PE

www.amberley-books.com

British Library Cataloguing in Publication Data.
A catalogue record for this book is available from the British Library.

ISBN 978 1 84868 463 8

Typesetting and origination by Amberley Publishing
Printed in Great Britain

CONTENTS

ABOUT THE AUTHOR

Ian Addicoat is an established writer and researcher of the paranormal and has been working in the field full time for the last ten years. He is president of The Paranormal Research Organisation (UK) and has investigated countless haunted properties, especially in the South West, adopting a rational and realistic approach to any apparent supernatural activity. He has appeared on various television programmes, including *Most Haunted*, *Animal X* and on GMTV. He is a partner in two companies, specialising in ghost walks and paranormal events, details of which are on the website www.ghosthunting.org.uk.

ACKNOWLEDGEMENTS

Photographs:
All photographs in the book were taken by myself, apart from those acknowledged otherwise. Special thanks for this go to Will Brunning, Amanda Hutchings and Shaun Markham.

Other Assistance:
I would especially like to thank all the publicans, staff members, pub visitors and other people who assisted me with this project with their stories and fascinating information. I am especially grateful to those fine people who have previously allowed my teams and myself to spend time investigating their properties, thus causing them loss of sleep and the inconvenience of a gang of investigators invading their haunted areas. I would also like to give special thanks to Debbie, Alishia and Connor, my mum and dad and all those fabulous friends who keep me insane (yes, I mean insane) with their love and shared laughter, you all know who you are and how much I appreciate all your contributions both to my work and especially to my soul!

INTRODUCTION

There are said to be over 50,000 public houses in the United Kingdom, and in many places a pub is an essential part of daily life, the focal point of the community. Samuel Pepys described the inn as the heart of England, and taverns, inns, bars, alehouses, hotels and pubs and their like have been an integral part of British culture since Roman times. The lives and dramas, intrigues and mysteries, deaths and traumas of the people who have visited pubs over the centuries are often part of the very fabric of the establishment, the drinkers having played out their roles in a kind of theatre of social alcohol consumption. As a result of such a rich tapestry of life, there are often many stories and histories that are inherently part of public houses, and, naturally, ghost stories and haunted reputations become a dynamic feature of such places. Pubs, more than any other location type, are frequently said to be haunted, and I have been collecting stories about haunted pubs for many years. While it would be easy to joke that it seems a great job for a paranormal investigator to spend his time frequenting pubs – an excuse for indulging in one too many 'spirits' – the reality is that such buildings genuinely do have the long history and frequency of visitors to make them the type of place more likely to have ghostly inhabitants. Indeed, if ghosts do exist then public houses are the very place you'd expect them to be and, well, if I ever get to choose a place to haunt then a pub might be just the place I would choose too!

I have always lived in the South West, and I have visited and stayed in countless haunted locations. I have sometimes been left with the impression of an altogether unexplained atmosphere, especially in pubs. The stories and accounts in this book are not meant to offer proof or overpowering evidence that ghosts exist but simply to supply fresh information and add personal accounts to ghost stories old and new.

Enjoy the book and visit as many of the pubs as you can to follow up the information and take in the atmosphere, it's always a good excuse to say you are there for research purposes!

CHAPTER 1

Admiral Benbow, Penzance, Cornwall

Halfway down the beautiful and historic Chapel Street in Penzance lies a unique seventeenth-century inn, named after the famous seventeenth-century Admiral John Benbow and also, of course, the title for the infamous hostelry in Treasure Island, fictional home to Jim Hawkins. The roof of the Admiral Benbow inn is resplendent with a large model of a smuggling figure, lying horizontal and holding a gun, and he has to be the one of the most photographed curiosities in the area. The inn was originally converted from an old cottage, and from the front the outside still has a quaint feel with its small windows and whitewashed walls. The pub was formerly owned by Roland Morris, a local diver, and still has a nautical theme. Many sea themed items, including, local wrecks (found and brought up off the notorious Cornish coast) items from canons and figureheads, decorate the inn. The pub's particularly unusual feature is, of course, the aforementioned attention-grabbing smuggler on the roof. This was modelled on a certain Octavius Lanyon, believed to have been the leader of a notorious eighteenth-century smuggling band who operated from the building. Legend has it that when the band of smugglers were caught by the revenue officers Octavius fled onto the roof, pitching his own version of Custer's last stand rather than face the inevitable trip to the gallows. Nevertheless, he was eventually captured and, presumably, executed. There are tunnels underneath the pub, which supports the claims of a smuggling heritage. Some of these tunnels remain today and people who have visited them over the years claim to have heard echoing footsteps approaching through the dark passageway, perhaps a ghostly resonance pertaining to the pub's smuggling past.

The Benbow is also alleged to be haunted by the ghost of a young lady, called either Anabelle or Arabella (the stories are inconsistent). She is believed to have lived here in the eighteenth century, dying of a broken heart when her lover was lost at sea. Many people over the years have claimed that they have experienced her presence, which has manifested itself in various ways. A story consistently attested for many years, I personally have known numerous people who have worked there and swear that it is haunted. Intriguingly, many of these people have only confessed that they believed the

Admiral Benbow, Penzance, Cornwall

Benbow to be haunted a long time after they left employment there, so presumably the claims have nothing to do with promoting the pub's haunted heritage. Other odd experiences have been described, including people feeling as though they are being watched and physical sensations, such as taps on the shoulder; interestingly, paranormal phenomena has been particularly observed in the pub's cellar. There have also been witnesses who claim to have seen a young woman's melancholy face, staring from an upstairs window. The interesting thing is that most of these witnesses apparently had no prior knowledge of the pub or story.

Acorn Inn, Evershot, Dorset

The Sow and Acorn in Thomas Hardy's *Tess of the D'Urbervilles* was based on this sixteenth-century coaching inn, nestling amongst the rolling hills close to the British Heritage Coastline in an area of outstanding natural beauty. This exquisite stone-built inn boasts a worthy history. Originally known as the Kings Arms, it once brewed its own ales with water drawn from the source of the River Frome. All the original charm and character of 400 years exudes from the beamed bars and log fires that greet guests on arrival.

A classic old British-style ghost, a sixteenth-century highwayman, reputedly haunts the Acorn Inn. The ghost is described almost like the caricature of a highwayman, with a flowing cape, three-cornered hat and black boots.

The Anchor Inn, Seatown, Dorset

Anchor Inn, Seatown, Dorset

Situated on the edge of the beach, this eighteenth-century pub is surrounded by beautiful National Trust land. The Anchor Inn at Seatown is rather unique, being situated amongst undulating hills and nestling under Golden Cap, the highest point on the south coast of England. The pub sits in the centre of a little cove with the South West Coast Path being all that separates the pub from the sands; unsurprisingly, there are many reported links between smuggling and the Anchor Inn.

The ghost of the Anchor Inn is said to be that of an excise man, stationed at the village guardhouse and employed to investigate local smugglers. He was shot dead at the top of the stairs leading up to the pub by a group of smugglers who'd been meeting in the inn and did not want to be prosecuted for their nefarious activities.

Angel Inn, Lyme Regis, Dorset

The Angel Inn is situated away from the town centre and has had reports based on their resident ghost for some years now. There are a few variations on the original story behind this spirit, but all seem to agree that the ghost of a former landlady, Mrs Langton, is responsible for the eerie sightings and mysterious movement of objects.

Mrs Langton was the landlady of the Angel Inn in 1926 and a very well-known local character. Some say her daughter was an alcoholic, something that brought Mrs Langton much distress during her lifetime and, presumably, was also enough to cause her spirit unrest once she was dead. Perhaps that is why she has continued to haunt the Angel Inn? A more widely believed theory, however, is that she was angry at being forced to leave 'her' pub while still alive. She is rumoured to have even placed a curse on the place, exclaiming that if she couldn't run her beloved pub no one else would do so successfully.

Interestingly, it is also alleged that Mrs Langton used to dress as Queen Victoria, hoping to bring herself an air of royalty. Although this seems an unlikely eccentricity, witnesses do, in fact, insist that the ghost of the Angel Inn does indeed look very much like Queen Victoria.

ANGEL HOTEL, HELSTON, CORNWALL

The Angel Hotel in central Helston dates back to the sixteenth century. It was once the town house of Lord Sidney Godolphin, the first minister to three monarchs and reputed to be one of the finest politicians in British history. Thereafter, it became a noted coaching inn and has been trading for over 250 years. The Angel Hotel is located on the main high street and is in a prime location to see the Furry Dance on Helston's famous Flora Day. The bar area was once the courtyard and still has a 40 ft well at its heart.

Local legend tells of the devil fighting with St Michael above the skies of west Cornwall and dropping a great stone to the ground. The stone was believed by many to be the one formerly used to block the entrance to hell and thus the name of the town, Helston, came into being. This black meta-gabbro stone landed behind the site of the hotel. The Angel is mooted to have been built from blocks hewn from this massive rock, which was broken up in the late eighteenth century and used in the hotel's west wall.

Traditionally the stone is said to bring bad luck to women who live at the inn. A number of strange things have also happened at the pub including peculiar noises, atmospheres, negative feelings and a shadowy form seen on numerous occasions.

Angel Inn, Lyme Regis, Dorset

CHAPTER 2

Bay Horse Inn, Ashburton, Devon

This is a welcoming, well-liked and traditional pub situated in North Street. It is said that the haunting manifestation here is linked to a child or perhaps a number of children. In the past, a variety of unexplained sounds have been heard, including the noise of running footsteps that sound unmistakably like a child's; this has happened when no child has actually been present. Other chilling noises heard here have included the melancholy sound of a girl sobbing. Tradition has it that these are the sobs of a youngster who caught diphtheria and died in this building.

There appears to be less paranormal activity at the Bay Horse Inn now than in previous years. However, the pub does certainly retain a palpably eerie atmosphere.

The Bay Horse Inn, Ashburton, Devon

The Bay Horse Inn, Totnes, Devon

Bay Horse Inn, Totnes, Devon

On an inclined street near the town centre, the inn is an eye-catching place, bedecked with window boxes and said to date back as far as 1485. It has a traditional vibe, though it is also bright, jovial and atmospheric. A man wearing a red coat is said to haunt the pub. He is small in physique and elderly and has been seen on a number of occasions. He usually disappears very swiftly and only certain people seem able to see him while at the same time others present are completely unaware that he's there. A few years ago a customer also claims to have been staying in one of the guest rooms when she was awoken by a strong feeling of being watched. On closer inspection she could make out a man with a straw hat moving across the room. He disappeared almost immediately and was not seen again.

Beehive Inn, Helston, Cornwall

This is a very popular pub and one of the main drinking establishments in Helston. It is open to the small hours (normally 3 a.m. on the weekends). The Beehive is long and narrow and has a dance floor, complete with a dance pole. As a result it can be very crowded, frequented by the usual groups of late-night revellers.

The most renowned ghost at the Beehive is the shadowy figure of man, aged about thirty and dressed in relatively modern clothing. Most sightings happen late at night, but they are only brief and it is never long before this mysterious chap disappears again.

He may be the ghost of a man murdered in the pub over 160 years ago, although the clothes might suggest otherwise. Some have suggested this may be a modern *doppelgänger*. Back in the 1980s the pub developed quite a reputation as a haunted venue after a local folk singer saw the ghostly figure of an old lady in a rocking chair in an upstairs room. He glanced away and on hearing a loud noise turned back to find that the old lady and the rocking chair had completely vanished into thin air.

Bell Inn, Kingsteignton, Devon

The Bell Inn, one of the oldest buildings in Kingsteignton, was built in the thirteenth century to accommodate the workers constructing the nearby church. The inn today prides itself on its relaxed atmosphere.

The wraith haunting this place is said to be a young girl murdered at the inn. Her screams have been heard reverberating across the hostelry, even when the pub stood empty and deserted.

Bishop Lacy Inn, Chudleigh, Devon

This is described as a quaint low-beamed church house dating back to the fourteenth century. An ecclesiastical figure in a cloak or robe is said to haunt the pub. It looks very much like a monk and is usually seen going up the stairs, where footsteps are also often heard. There has been widespread poltergeist activity, said to be down to the clerical spook and particularly common during changes of tenancy. This activity has included beer taps being turned on, kettles being boiled and other phenomena.

People claim this is the ghost of Edmund Lacey who was bishop of Exeter until his death at Chudleigh on 18 September 1455 and after whom the pub is named. The bishop used the building as a summerhouse and it was part of a wider monastery complex. Numerous miracles were said to have taken place at his tomb, which is at the north side of the cathedral choir. It remains a common story that Lacey was the only one of the bishops of Exeter to whom any reputation of unusual sacredness was attached after death. There have also been sightings of a mysterious Victorian lady with white hair and wearing a white dress at the pub.

Bowl Inn, Lower Almondsbury, Bristol

The Bowl Inn is a very historic public house, nestled on the south-east edge of the Severn Vale, in the village of Lower Almondsbury. The Bowl Inn derives its name from the shape of the land surrounding the Severn Estuary, which can be seen from the inn. Parts of this picturesque, whitewashed stone inn were originally the three cottages erected in 1146 to house the monks who were building the adjacent Church of St Mary the Virgin. During subsequent centuries, the tunnels between these cottages, the church and priory (now a farmhouse) were created to afford protection against marauding foreign invaders. The present building became a licensed inn in 1550 and James II's sheriffs used it during the latter half of the seventeenth century to give trial to supporters of the Duke of Monmouth.

The pub has several reported ghosts, the most famously attested to being that of a young French girl called Elizabeth Maronne who died at the hands of her wicked father in 1708. She is often seen and heard crying in the village, as well as being heard reciting nursery rhymes. The most recent, firm sighting was as recently as the late 1970s. A plaque inside the local church tells us that her father believed his children (Elizabeth and her brother John) died because of his sins. There are also said to be two other female ghosts that haunt the pub, but nothing is known about them. Interestingly there is rumoured to be a sealed passageway from the Bowl Inn to the church, said to be haunted by a monk and a black bear.

Bucket of Blood Pub, Hayle, Cornwall

This alarmingly titled inn near Hayle has a great deal of fascinating history. It is linked to ghostly activity and a notorious legend; nothing can be more disturbing than the myth that reputedly gave this pub its name. From early times there has been a pub here, supposedly a previous haven for pirates, smugglers, sailors and the like. A deep well served the inn at one time, and one morning several centuries ago the then landlord went to raise the bucket to collect water. As he brought up the pail he realised that not water but blood was in the bucket. Later, a search discovered a badly mutilated body at the bottom of the well. This is claimed to have been a revenue officer who had been investigating smuggling activity in the area. The truth may never be known – but it certainly is a macabre story.

There are several ghost stories attached to the place including ghostly figures seen crossing the road outside, footsteps moving across the creaking floorboards upstairs and many other strange occurrences besides.

What better place than this for a paranormal investigation? In 2003 I accompanied

Bucket of Blood Pub, Hayle, Cornwall

a team of fellow investigators from the Paranormal Research Organisation (P.R.O.), of which I am president, on an investigation here and in the nearby graveyard. On this occasion the research team was comprised of a mixture of psychics and sceptics.

The psychic team, who had no prior knowledge of the building, came up with some intriguing information. A male presence in his forties (and who had apparently been murdered in the cellar) was identified by the team. Allegedly, he exits the pub via the cellar door and crosses the road where he then moves through the hedge opposite the pub. He may well have been a previous landlord, and dowsing results revealed that he might have been called Bernard. The presence of a young teenage male was also sensed. He was not believed by the psychic team to be linked to the pub but rather to the land surrounding it where a number of the team developed feelings of sadness and loneliness. The presence of an old woman in the bar was picked up on, and although the person who witnessed her was unsure of her exact age, she was identified as being well into her eighties. She had possibly lived down the road nearby and was linked to the area. A cat and a dog were picked up in an outside garage, perhaps linked to the stable that was previously situated there. The presence of a one-eyed man called Jack, aged in his seventies, a sexton and regular to the pub, was also sensed by the psychic team. The presence of an elderly man and woman were identified, they were not regulars to the pub and, in actual fact, apparently linked to the landlord not the pub. Twin nine-year-old girls were identified in the bar area and in the same area several investigators caught the unpleasant aroma of dead rabbits.

At the end of the investigation, the results were discussed with the landlord and much of the information picked up on by the team's psychics seemed to be accurate when compared to the pub's history and previously reported paranormal activity, despite, as always, the team not being allowed access to any information about the pub before the investigation.

The most exciting discovery was probably the news that a man called Jack, who had only had one eye, used to drink here in recent years. He apparently came to the pub every night until he died in 1972. He would sit in a particular chair, this being exactly where our psychic had sensed his presence. Furthermore his photo was provided and matched the descriptions given to a staggering degree of similarity! The landlord later confirmed that this man Jack had indeed been the sexton for the churchyard next door.

It also seems that a former landlady, Mrs Chandler, is sometimes seen, as is a landlord. Interestingly, the spot where the team smelt dead rabbits appeared to relate to a true fact. There had been a hunter who had frequented the pub and who would often sit in the pub with captured rabbits hanging from his belt. The two nine-year-old girls were also sensed in an area where people have previously sensed a presence.

After the investigation of the pub several intrepid volunteers, including myself, headed off into the graveyard nearby to search for a monk who is apparently sited here. Oddly, during the visit one camera failed to work and another refused to turn off. A stone in the churchyard has been sited here for 1,500 years and many people from the nearby estate have claimed that a monk is seen walking nearby. The ghostly figure was apparently seen by quite a number of witnesses, including the sexton Jack (above) and dogs are often known to play up in this particular area!

There is rumoured to be a large smuggler's tunnel under the building that runs from opposite the garage, which was formerly a stable. It appears to be separate to the pub and is more likely to have been used for smuggling than as a mining tunnel.

BULL HOTEL, BRIDPORT, DORSET

Easy-going, informal and bursting with life, this former seventeenth-century coaching inn, lovingly restored, oozes eclectic style and contemporary-rustic charm. However, in 1645, during the ill-fated Monmouth Rebellion, the Bull Inn was the scene of a skirmish. A troop of Monmouth's men under Colonel Venner entered the town and shots were fired from the Bull. In the fight that followed, Edward Coker of Mapperton and Wadham Strangways were killed. In 1849 the Bull was sold to the Knight family, remaining under the family's possession for the next 110 years. It was rebuilt with a ballroom, minstrels' gallery and billiard room, complete with the plaque of 1877 proudly stating it to be the 'Knight's Bull Hotel'.

The faint sounds of a child are heard here, more often than not in the ladies' toilets. The area has then been investigated by members of the public and members of staff, but no toddler is ever found. An ethereal woman in tweed is also said to sit in the reception area.

Bush Inn, Morwenstow, Cornwall

The Bush Inn at Morwenstow is a thirteenth-century free house in a dramatic location just off the South West Coast Path between Bude and Hartland, on what has to be one of the most spectacular stretches of the Cornish coast. Once a haunt for smugglers and wreckers, the historic inn has provided nourishment for weary travellers for hundreds of years, possibly dating back to AD 950. It is believed at that time to have been a monk's rest for those on the pilgrimage route from Wales to Spain who crossed Cornwall between the North Devon ports and Fowey.

In the main bar is a Celtic piscina cut from serpentine stone and a monastic cross, carved into the flagstone floor. Situated in the middle bar is the 'Leper's Squint', a tiny window through which scraps of food were passed to the deprived of the parish and later used as a lookout for the wreckers and smugglers who operated on this treacherous part of the coastline. The most infamous smuggler on this part of the coast was Cruel Coppinger, a notorious, sadistic individual who came ashore at Welcombe Mouth in 1792, the sole survivor of a wrecked Danish vessel. He operated along this stretch of coast with his gang of cut-throats and such was their reputation that even the Revenue Officers avoided them.

The Bush Inn has had a haunted reputation for many years and was featured, over twenty years ago, in a BBC Radio Cornwall programme. The broadcasts were produced with investigator and author Michael Williams and strange noises were recorded and heard. There have been a number of previous sightings at the pub including in 1968 a strange dark shadowy figure being seen at the time of an unfortunate fire at the pub. Also a salty old sailor clad in very dated clothing has been seen disappearing through a wall. A multitude of peculiar noises have been heard and other peculiar events taken place at the Bush. These include: footsteps sounding on the staircase; noises like a door being knocked in an area where there is no door; clicking, thudding and banging sounds; animals playing up; sudden drops in temperature; a door being continually opened, even when wire was wrapped around the catch; and an unexplained oppressive atmosphere.

CHAPTER 3

Cannard's Well Inn, Shepton Mallet, Somerset

The village is named after Tom Kennard, the last man in England to be hanged for sheep stealing. The pub stands at the intersection of several roads and used to be the Cannard's Grave Inn. It originally had a gibbet as an inn sign, but, in the 1990s, the name was softened to the Cannards Well Hotel and the sign was changed, as it disturbed many a potential visitor.

Tom Kennard, often called either Giles Cannard, or Tom the Taverner, was the landlord of a public house, which stood on the crossroads of several roads. Opposite the inn, as was usual at such crossroads, stood a grim reminder of the relative lawlessness of those times, a gibbet, on which smugglers, highwaymen, bandits and other criminals met their ends.

Tom's tavern was popular because he allegedly provided a sanctuary to a number of such local mischief-makers. He was rumoured to have identified guests with riches, selling the information to would-be thieves. A few miles away from the inn the poor travellers would find themselves robbed, never aware of the landlord's connivance. Eventually, according to legend, some merchants accused Tom of such misdeeds. However, no action was taken and as a result the merchants organised a mob and went as a group to the inn with the objective of lynching Tom. The petrified Tom escaped but committed suicide by hanging himself from the nearby gibbet. An alternative version of the story claims that Tom was a highwayman in league with the notorious Dr Syn, the Scarecrow of Romney Marsh. However, his dishonest profession ended when he was discovered with ten stolen sheep in his yard and he was found guilty and hanged from the gibbet. The tavern fell into decline and a restaurant stands on the spot. The gibbet was eventually removed and the current pub was built in its place.

There have been numerous reports of the pub and surrounding area being haunted. The earliest is from the Reverend H. Allen, rector of Shepton Mallet, who wrote in 1692, 'the soul could not rest and frequently visits the scenes of its former abode while in the flesh'. Apparently there have been a number of encounters over the years, especially on dark and stormy nights.

Castle Inn, St Ives, Cornwall

Castle Inn, St Ives, Cornwall

This pub, often described by locals as definitely the best pub in town, especially if you're after real ale, is reputedly haunted by Maud, a prostitute who allegedly resided in the building at the beginning of the twentieth century. In particular, she is active in the cellar areas of the pub and also in the back rooms where her rented space was apparently situated. She has been up to all kinds of mischievous pranks over the years and several independent landlords have confirmed their belief that the pub is haunted. Some of the antics associated with her misbehaviour have included doors mysteriously opening by themselves, objects being moved and turning up in peculiar places and things going wrong with the barrels of beer. In particular, clips left on real ale barrels often go missing and usually turn up in the bin, which is completely on the opposite end of the bar. They have also been known to turn up in other unlikely places.

Many of the locals are fully aware of Maud's ghostly presence, especially in the loos, where she is often claimed to play with hand dryers and other electrical products.

Castle of Comfort Hotel, Dodington, Somerset

The Castle of Comfort, which is a Grade II listed building, is believed to date from the sixteenth century or possibly even earlier. It was a coaching inn during the seventeenth century, after which it became a coffee house and then a cider house when copper mining took place in the area. Miners collected their wages from the counting house just to the east and came down to the Castle of Comfort for refreshment.

In February 2005 I was part of a small P.R.O. team that planned to spend the whole night investigating this fantastic property. The first thing that needs to be said is what a delightful and beautiful hotel it is and it was difficult to believe that such a pleasant property could possibly be haunted. However, it might just be that we were very wrong!

The investigation was carried out entirely indoors, and we were left on our own whilst the owners retired, leaving the building fully locked off and under our control. The evening began quietly, apart from some orbs being photographed. However, as the evening progressed more and more happened. At one stage, as the team were apparently communicating with a presence, the most incredible orbs were appearing on the night vision camera and for an extended period these seemed to be responding to the team on cue. Although I am very sceptical of orbs this did seem rather intriguing.

Overall, a lot of information was picked up and, as we had solitary access to the whole hotel, there was plenty of opportunity to explore and investigate. Given that, due to unforeseen circumstances, the team only consisted of four members, we had our work cut out to investigate each room, so we focused on those rooms where the most paranormal activity had been previously experienced. However, each room was investigated and the high level of results might support the theory that more supernatural activity is likely to occur to individuals or smaller groups.

In the Mariner Room, the team sensed a thirteen-year-old servant girl called Rebecca who died in 1800 and who runs back and forth in the room. Also there was another female presence named Sarah Gray whose room this had been. She had been aged twenty-seven or twenty-eight when she had fallen down some stairs to her death. When we returned to this room at 3.50 a.m. the spirit identified as Rebecca was still there. One investigator felt tingling in the back of his throat and thought Rebecca was trying to speak through him and then felt as if he could see her standing in front of him about 3ft away. He described her as having shoulder-length curly brown hair and wearing a navy-blue dress with a white pinafore.

In the Italian Room – the room that is supposedly the most active – the team picked up on a presence moving back and forth between the two foot-ends of the bed. This was a female named Tilly who, it seems, shows herself and moves things.

In the Tintern Room there was an unfriendly male presence in his fifties. He had died in 1916. A story then emerged that his wife had died shortly after they had been married by falling down a well. The male presence claimed that she had been pushed but that it had not been him, although he had been accused of it at the time.

In the hotel's dining room, my colleague was led by the dowsing rods to the radiator and felt icy cold. The radiator is to the side of the old fireplace and was turned on.

When I went to check for a cold spot both my colleague and I felt a tingling sensation and the hairs on our arms stood up. Another investigator then also felt this and whilst dowsing identified two spirits in the area. The first was a little girl aged nine who died in 1934. She was unable to give a name as she was not capable of reading or writing but she did convey to the team that she had died of natural causes. The second presence was a man who was standing by the fireplace. His name was George Brent and he died in the Middle East in 1842. He told us that he was a sergeant in the army infantry based at Jellalabad barracks in Taunton, and the majority of his company were killed in one battle where he had been tragically beheaded. Because we had information on George Brent and his commanding officer we decided to conduct some research. After the investigation we began looking on the Internet at the light infantry's historic battles. It was amazing for us to find the following piece detailing a battle with a massive death toll that took place in Jellalabad, 1842, under the commanding officer Sir Robert Sale. Our psychic's information had been remarkably close to the facts and we can only wonder if he genuinely communicated with a former soldier.

The year 1841 in Kabul began in peace but was destined to end in disaster. Although the British were optimistic for the future, there were indications that Afghanistan was, beneath the surface, seething with discontent, and the invaders, the British, were, in reality, hated. On 13 January 1842 the worst anticipations of the garrison at Jellalabad were fulfilled. Captain Henry Havelock described the following:

> About 2pm on 13 January some officers were assembled on the roof of the loftiest house in Jellalabad. One of them espied a single horseman riding towards our walls. As he got nearer it was distinctly seen that he wore European clothes and was mounted on a travel-hacked yaboo, which he was urging on with all the speed of which it yet remained master. A signal was made to him by someone on the walls which he answered by waving a private soldier's forage cap over his head. The Kabul gate was thrown open, and several officers rushing out, received and recognised in the traveller, who dismounted, the first and it is to be feared, the last fugitive of the ill-fated force at Kabul, Dr Brydon.

The arrival of Dr Brydon at Jellalabad has been immortalised by Lady Butler's famous picture, 'The Remnants of an Army'. He was the sole survivor of an army of 4,550 fighting men and 12,000 followers to reach Jellalabad, though there were about 100 captives, including women and children, in the hands of the enemy.

Choughs Hotel,
Chard, Somerset

CHOUGHS HOTEL, CHARD, SOMERSET

In 1685, Chard was one of the towns that Judge Jeffreys appeared in after the failure of the Monmouth Rebellion, in order to hold some of the Bloody Assizes. Charles I's men marched through Chard and it is here that Monmouth rallied his troops. Many a man was hung at the old oak tree here in the village. It is stated that the infamous judge and baron stayed in the Choughs Hotel and passed out his harsh judgements from an impromptu court in the building. There have been several secret passageways discovered and other built-in oddities in a building which has hardly changed since those harrowing times. The pub has a tombstone behind a fireplace and a mummified chough bird in a tiny coffin.

There are four recorded ghosts, including the wicked wraith of Judge Jeffreys, who it seems, by the number of locations he apparently haunts, must be a very busy ghost indeed. There is a room upstairs known as Jeffreys' Room, where his coat of arms is displayed on the wall. His manifestations here at the Chough are described in terms of the image of a grim, evil-faced chap who walks in an upstairs room and is occasionally witnessed crouching to the right of the main fireplace. Phantom voices of female origin and also the sound of whispering and soft laughter have been heard in another room and the ghost of an elderly lady witnessed. There is another voice that seems to be angry with this female presence, and the appearance of this angry voice is often followed by slamming doors. The room in question had probably been a ladies' room. One previous landlord claimed that a guest had once come out of that room in a panic and left the hotel immediately. He had been in the room when he had suddenly felt a sharp pain on his face and the landlord claimed that he could actually see a visible red mark. The third ghost is of a man in a suit of armour, with chains dangling from his ankles and wrists. He is seen and heard clanking along, but vanishes when anyone approaches him. The fourth ghost is that of a little old lady who has been glimpsed moving along a corridor at the back of the building. Also, poltergeist activity has occurred, including glasses landing on the floor (amazingly, these are found unbroken despite having fallen from high shelves). Other shadowy forms have been seen moving around, including a figure seen passing by a window in the yard, and there are often electrical problems, especially with equipment, and objects have been known to move.

The pub was the location for an investigation by a Bristol-based paranormal group in 2007 but, unfortunately, they concluded that it was not a terribly active night.

Clock House Inn, Chideock, Dorset

The Clock House Hotel is a thatched 400-year-old country pub where a former landlord and his wife attested to seeing a ghost in the car park. They described this apparition as a (literally) legless lady. Desperately trying to avoid the obvious pun, I will just add that a black dog and a priest wearing black garments also, it is said, haunt the nearby road and churchyard.

Clock House Inn, Chideock, Dorset

Coach and Horses, Buckland Brewer, Devon

The Coach and Horses, built in the thirteenth century, was once a busy coaching house on the old thoroughfare from Bideford to Holsworthy. The thatched two-storey inn still retains its low-beamed ceilings and olde-worlde charm. In the seventeenth or eighteenth century it is reputed that the inn was used as a courtroom, the cellars adapted as a gaol and an execution drop situated in a room above the main bar (the unfortunate people who were executed then dropping into the court room below). There were once said to have been rings in the ceiling beams, to which the prisoner's wrists were fastened. One of the presiding judges was believed to have been the infamous Judge Jeffreys. Originally there was an inn, coach house, stables and shop (all thatched) set around a cobbled courtyard. The stables, coach house and shop were unfortunately destroyed in a fire in the early 1920s. The stables were never rebuilt but a garage replaced the coach house and shop.

With such a nefarious reputation it is perhaps not surprising that the pub lays claim to ghostly activity. A lady in black has been witnessed moving along a corridor and in various rooms in the lower part of the pub. Shadowy figures have been witnessed upstairs and footsteps have been heard when it is known that the area is empty, particularly in the area where the trap hatch had been. The pub is also said to be haunted by ghosts from an earlier time, namely those of two cavalier soldiers standing where the old execution trap door was and a roundhead in one of the bedrooms. This is feasible as there were a number of known Civil War skirmishes in the area around the pub.

Coach and Horses, Rosudgeon, Cornwall

Built in about 1750, with later extensions in the nineteenth and twentieth centuries, it was, as the name suggests, built as a coaching inn. The pub has recently re-launched and is a fine example of a good warm local pub serving home style cooking. The decor is cosy and the welcome is friendly.

In 2004 I took a small team of investigators with the Paranormal Research Organisation to investigate this pub and it proved to be a very rewarding night, with one member of the team in particular proving to be very adept with a pair of dowsing rods. He proceeded to actually obtain some incredibly accurate information about the building's history, previous paranormal activity and even things that were personal to the family that run the pub and could not have been previously researched.

First of all, our psychic picked up on a male presence in the bar, hanging around by the fireplace. He was a man who had died in his fifties and had worked in the building

The Coach and Horses, Rosudgeon, Cornwall

from the late 1790s up until his death in the early 1840s. Then he identified a female presence called Henrietta, who had been, it transpired, the wife of the aforementioned male, the two of them being tenant landlord and lady. She had died in her mid-forties when she fell to her death after tripping and falling. A third presence was that of a little boy aged five or six, son of the above two. He apparently carries out mischief in the family room and is often heard knocking on tables. He had sadly died after being hit on the road outside by a horse and cart. The fourth presence sensed by my investigation team was a gentleman who had owned the building in the mid-eighteenth century. He apparently has the demeanour of someone who believes that they are still in charge. He is the person responsible for poltergeist activity in the bar and indeed items such as glasses and ornaments have often moved by themselves. Interestingly, this figure has been seen by numerous witnesses over the years. Next, our psychic picked up on a lady from the 1940s, who she thought had a proclivity for touching the grandfather clock located in the bar area. Significantly, we later discovered that there have been numerous occasions that this clock has chimed at the wrong time or inexplicably jammed. Behind the bar the presence of a former barman was also sensed by the investigation team. They discovered that he was called Christian Godfrey and he had gone off to war in the 1940s. He had died many years later at the age of sixty-five. As well as these presences, the team also picked up on a terrier dog, seemingly owned by Christian, and three horses outside. Indeed, according to the family that runs the pub, horses' hoof beats previously been heard here.

Coombe Cellars Pub, Combeinteignhead, Devon

This is a traditional village pub sited at Combeinteignhead, an old settlement on the southern bank of the Teign Estuary. For centuries Combeinteignhead and the Coombe Cellars was a wild and remote place frequented only by locals and smugglers. The present riverside pub, now much altered, is believed to date from the seventeenth century and may at one time have been called the Ferry Inn. Contraband used to be dropped off here in the eighteenth century.

There is one particular bedroom in which it is rumoured that a lady haunted the area. She is located in one main part of the bedroom and people often get a feeling as if somebody is wandering around the room. One possibility is that this is the ghost of a young woman from London who was murdered at the inn by a burglar, back in the eighteenth century. It has been known for a guest to awake feeling as if they are being strangled. Remarkably a painting was found and purchased revealing the very same scene and what looked to be same room. Alternatively, it has been suggested that this might instead be the ghost of Emma, Lady Hamilton, who is best remembered as the mistress of Lord Nelson and as the muse of George Romney and who is known to have met with the admiral here.

Cornish Arms, Redruth, Cornwall

In May 2005 the Paranormal Research Organisation carried out an investigation at this pleasant pub, a former coaching inn. This was an investigation for which the landlady had specifically invited us. Apparently, strange activity was said to have been very prevalent at the Cornish Arms and so we arrived with eager anticipation of the night ahead, thinking that perhaps if we had not been part of a professional investigation we would surely have enjoyed a few drinks and the atmosphere of this very old pub. Unfortunately, however, it was a relatively disappointing evening in terms of paranormal activity, which may have been in no small part to the large number of non-members who had been invited along by the landlady. We made every effort to continue our research but unfortunately the large number of people and their levels of excitement proved detrimental to any meaningful investigation techniques. We did, however, get a very interesting photograph of a coloured streak leading towards my throat. I think this is most likely to be a colour spread caused by the movement of the camera, though one other investigator jokingly suggested it was a ghost going for my throat. I definitely prefer to think that it was a camera fault, though we did experience several incidents of unexplained battery drainage during the night!

In the Doom Bar, named after a notorious local sandbank where many ships have been wrecked, our psychic did identify a male who had died in 1718, aged fifty, and suggested that he likes to move things and to play with the lantern. Significantly, we later discovered that this was a part of the pub where people visiting have seen a lantern moving from side to side. We were also told that in the subsequent days after our visit, paranormal activity in the pub rose dramatically, with some very peculiar goings on.

Cornish Arms Hotel, St Blazey, Par, Cornwall

Dating back over 200 years, the Cornish Arms Hotel is a delightful old Georgian coaching inn that has an impressive columned doorway. The stable block has been discerningly converted into accommodation rooms. The interior of the pub has been extensively renovated and is therefore modern in appearance with a quasi Art Deco style.

It is believed that the area where the building stands today and surrounding the churchyard saw a great deal of activity during the time of the English Revolution, with frequent skirmishes between Royalist and Parliamentarian troops occurring.

The public house is situated on the main A390 next to the churchyard, which is also believed to be haunted. It has a large accommodation area where I have investigated a number of times, including during some ghost nights held for the public when our guests have claimed to have witnessed a ghostly figure and all sorts of other strange phenomena (see www.ghosthunting.org.uk). Over the years, many rooms of the Cornish Arms have been the sites of alleged supernatural and unexplained activity.

The Cornish Arms has been featured in the local media for its paranormal activity and there has been a great deal of consistently reported information. People have heard unexplained noises and witnesses have seen ghostly figures, apparitions, moving shadows, sudden flashes of light and many other peculiar sights. A ghostly horse and carriage is said to pass through the village stopping at the Cornish Arms and people are said to hear the clattering of hooves and feel a strong breeze as it passes by, though it is rarely seen. The ghostly figure of a man who loved the place in his time still frequents the bar area and there have been numerous reports of poltergeist activity in the bar, including bottles and glasses moving. Cigar smoke has been smelt in the restaurant area and, needless to say, people do not smoke anymore in that area. Cutlery and candles have also been mysteriously interfered with, and the sound of barrels has often been heard in the cellars when nobody is there.

A few months ago the pub hit the local media after a visit by a local medium called Gayle Force and her encounter with a bottom-pinching chef in the kitchen area. Several newspapers, radio and TV stations reported what had happened and our local TV station filmed a séance that took place in the cellar.

After one of the ghost nights I organised at the pub, I received the following correspondence from an attendee:

> Hi Ian, Thank you so much for a truly memorable evening at the above venue. I thoroughly enjoyed it and look forward to many more of your evenings. Once again, many thanks for what did turn out to be a truly memorable night, during which I am sure I saw my first 'ghost'. Certainly made my hair stand on end because I apologised to him – or at least to the disappearing coat tail and leg of him! He was in the bathroom of room No. 7 and I caught a glimpse of him as he disappeared from my view inside the bathroom going to the left of the open door as I looked toward the bathroom because the light was on. I apologised because I thought we'd walked into a room that was occupied! Well, it was, but not by a living entity! I wish I'd had my camera ready because I know I didn't imagine him! Wow, what an evening. We even managed a really informative séance. Also, I don't know what the history is with room No. 8 – but it certainly had a creepy/oppressed feel to it that doesn't lend itself to a good nights sleep! It has certainly whetted my appetite for long-term continued investigation of the paranormal. I can't wait for the next serving.

In the hallway people attending the ghost nights have picked up on a feeling of being watched and one person had the feeling that a big disaster involving many deaths had happened here. In room No. 8 one person began to try to pick up information psychically and brought forth information about a young female. She was apparently aged seventeen and had died in 1846. Her name was Elizabeth and she had worked here. The person further reported that she had died unlawfully and that her position was near to the door. Later a lady felt her wrap being pulled. In room No. 9 other attendees have picked up on a young male and a young female has also been identified, and people have heard knocking, a girl's voice and the sound of a cat. One group previously heard a large noise like barrels being dropped but it turned out to be the gate outside. However, as they returned, one person saw something like a dark shadow manifest at the end of the corridor.

Cowick Barton Inn, Exeter

This inn is thought to have been built on the site of the Cowick priory in the late sixteenth century, and it may well have been the priory farm mentioned in the Domesday Book. The building was built by Lord John Russell and was used as a hunting lodge following the Dissolution of the Monasteries under the reign of Henry VIII. The building was later used as a house and acquired by the White-Abbott family who resided there between 1763 and 1851. Numerous other owners lived there until in 1963 the brewery purchased the then derelict property and turned it into the Cowick Barton Inn.

The pub's most famous ghost is, not surprisingly, that of a monk. He is said to be a benevolent fellow who particularly appears at times when people residing in the house are ill; he is believed to be trying to assist them. People have positive feelings about him and he is most often seen wearing dark robes, appearing through the front entrance and moving across the lounge. A similar figure has also been seen in nearby houses and in a field in close proximity to the river, all of which would have formerly been monastery land.

The inn's other ghost is said to be that of a Royalist soldier, appearing in the bedrooms. A number of people have awoken to find him lent over them as if observing them but, again, nobody reports anything negative about him.

CROW'S NEST INN, PORT ISAAC, CORNWALL

This quaint inn was built in the late nineteenth century as two private houses and lies underneath Caradon Hill, overlooking Port Isaac Bay. It is aptly titled as it is situated on the cliff top with amazing views out to Tintagel Head. It was turned into a hotel and then, in 1985, a pub called the Shipwrights Arms but it changed name again in 2000. The large picture windows in the bar allow majestic views from inside.

In February 2009 a young couple came and had lunch in the bar and claimed to have had a very strange experience. The lady felt as if someone had walked behind her, brushing past her back and she then also felt a tap on her back. She looked behind her, expecting to see the waitress clearing up, but no one was there. She looked back at her boyfriend, who was as white as a sheet because he had seen *something* behind her. As they finished their lunch she looked over at the cushions in front of the window and saw a peculiar shimmering. At this point the lady became very nervous, so the couple left soon after. They both wondered if the pub was known to be haunted but had no prior knowledge whatsoever.

Curiously, the pub does allegedly have several ghosts. First of all there is a grey haired lady in nineteenth-century clothing seen walking through what had once been a window in the dining room. Also there are said to be the ghosts of a young mining boy and a bride waiting for her miner lover to return from work. Interestingly, there are said to be links between the pub and the local mine. Furthermore, there is a gentleman who allegedly walks through the bar, sometimes appearing as an indistinct shadow. This apparition has been linked to glasses being smashed and unexplained footsteps on the staircase when nobody is there.

Crumplehorn Inn, Polperro, Cornwall

The Crumplehorn Inn and Watermill used to be a farm; although the mill dates from the fourteenth century it only became an inn in 1972. The inn also used to be a counting house back in Elizabethan times when privateering was a legal profession. Ships' captains could legally rob Spanish and French ships and split the profits with the Crown. The Crown's part went to fund the navy in further attacks against the foreign fleets. The mill's alehouse was also home to Zephaniah Job, who was known as the 'smuggler's banker' and even issued his own banknotes, one of which is displayed at Truro Museum.

A few years ago I was in regular communication with the then landlord Andrew Taylor, who was kind enough to keep me up-to-date with paranormal events at the pub. As far as the ghosts are concerned there are claimed to be a few! One seems to frequent the bar and people usually just manage catch a glimpse of something out of the corner of their eye. A few years ago, however, a relation of the landlord was working in the bar one Sunday evening and had a strange experience when she thought everyone was out of the bar. She turned the lights off and headed for the kitchen, and as she went past the door to the toilets, the door opened all the way (it has a spring closer and doesn't open easily). Thinking she had locked someone in, she said 'sorry, I thought every one was out'. The door to the toilets then closed, so she went in only to find that there was no one there. Significantly, all the windows were closed and there was no wind.

In one flat, which is situated in the fourteenth-century part of the inn, there is allegedly a ghost that turns on lights during the night. One guest was sitting on the end of the bed when she saw someone go into the bathroom. She thought it was one of her children and asked if they were OK but there was no reply and when she went into the bathroom there was no one there. One night during her stay she woke up to find all the lights on in the lounge, the hallway, the bathroom and even a table standard lamp. A member of staff also stayed there and woke up one night to find the light in the hallway on.

In early November 2001 the inn was visited by The Ghost Research Foundation and three researchers stayed overnight in the same apartment. When they went upstairs to check on one of their cameras, the hall light had been turned on, and when they awoke in the morning the window in the bedroom had been opened. More unexplained paranormal activity was reported in August 2001 when a couple stayed here. One night they awoke to find the front door wide open and the window in the twin-bedded room open also. On another occasion, they woke to find that all the lights were on in the lounge, hall, bathroom and toilet. The man also woke alone one morning in the double-bedded room feeling freezing cold; he recalled seeing his frosty breath when he breathed out. But this was August week and there had been high daytime temperatures and mild nights!

Another incident occurred when a friend of the landlord was at the inn one night. He awoke to see a small woman in a flowery dress leaning over the bed. She looked at him, frowned and then disappeared.

One of the strangest incidents occurred in the landlord's own accommodation, the sixteenth-century mill house. He woke up one morning as it was getting light and saw someone standing in front of the mirror with a cigarette in their hand and clasping their forehead as though they had a really bad headache. The landlord thought it must be his wife and asked if she was OK but there was no answer, so he said 'are you all right?' The person, however, didn't move, so he looked to his left and was astounded to see his wife in bed next to him. When he looked up the apparition was gone. He examined the room to see if there was anything that he could have misinterpreted but there was not. His late wife was a very psychic lady and on a number of occasions they heard, coming from the Mill loft, what sounded like a man and a woman whispering. Then one night they also heard the sound of a door latching, even though there is no door in the loft. His wife thought it was a soldier from the First World War who had hidden in the attic with his lover and was later killed in the trenches.

I also received the following email from someone who had stayed in the inn just a few years ago:

> My partner and I stayed at the inn on Friday night (14 Jan) with her sister and sister's boyfriend, we had the adjoining flats 1 and 4 and some strange things occurred. We went out for a meal in the village and returned about midnight with the intention of sitting up for a while over a few drinks but when we all got back to flat 4, the two girls were violently sick. At around five in the morning there was a sound of metal being dragged across the draining board in the kitchen area and my girlfriend's sister's jewellery had disappeared. We all heard a coffee cup move, when no one was around or near the kitchen area! When we checked out and drove away from the inn my girlfriend felt better and was no longer sick. Us boys were not ill in any way, although we all ate similar things.

He was quite convinced that this was as a result of something paranormal.

In 2004 I was part of a team from the Paranormal Research Organisation to investigate the building overnight and we did experience some interesting results. First of all my team went into an area in the grounds said to have once been a drover's path to see if we could pick up anything. My colleague picked up on a very unfriendly male in his thirties who seemed to follow us around the area. His name was said to be Joe and apparently Crumplehorn used to be a farm and mill at the time of his death in 1659. He had apparently been strangled and through a long process of questions with 'yes' and 'no' answers we built up the story that he had fallen in love with a local girl (not reciprocated) and had sexually attacked her and so her husband had killed him in revenge. Interestingly when the other group came here, without any knowledge of our experiences, they also picked up on a man who was not friendly and had been murdered because he had done a wrong deed, although they did not find out what this was. He apparently said that he did not think that he deserved to die and that he also stole something that did not belong to him.

We then began to investigate flat No. 4. Before we began, however, I removed a picture known as the Pink Fisherman from the wall because in the past paranormal activity has apparently increased when it is moved. Our dowser then picked up on two main presences. Firstly there was a woman named Sarah aged in her thirties. She had been married to a farmer and they both worked here. She had died because of a tragic accident in 1812, relating to farm machinery and a horse, perhaps something falling onto her from a cart, and had died two or three days later as a result. The second presence was her sister Daeliah. She had apparently been of Welsh origin and older than Sarah. She had apparently not been happy with her sister, which was something to do with her sister's husband. There may have even been a family feud because Sarah's family they felt she was too good for her husband. The other team also independently picked up on two females who were related and further identified a male fisherman who was sixty-seven years old when he died of an accident. He did not die in the building but the pub was his local.

We then headed to the main bar and restaurant areas. Here the dowsing team identified three presences: two men and one woman, a dog and a goat. The female was happy and had lived at the inn, dying aged forty-six or forty-seven and was a servant. One male presence was not willing to talk but the second male by the bar communicated that he had died aged fifty-eight in about 1675. He did not live here but nearby and worked as a farmer.

Crystal Palace Tavern, Bath, Somerset

With its wondrous setting and rich history, the Crystal Palace Tavern, formerly known as the Three Tuns, is very popular with locals, tourists and students alike. It was renamed in the 1860s in honour of The Great Exhibition. During a renovation years ago, a Roman pavement was discovered in the cellar, alongside some human bones, believed to be part of a monastic graveyard.

Consistently with the monk's graveyard, the ghostly apparition seen here is of a figure in a cowled hood. One such sighting even coincided with the discovery of the bones.

CHAPTER 4

Dartmoor Inn, Lydford, Devon

Just before you turn off the main road to head towards Lydford, you pass the sixteenth-century Dartmoor Inn. This place is full of character and atmosphere and is a former coaching inn. This is a pub that seems to back up the idea that ghosts tend to play up when things change in their place of residence. Here it seems that a phantom manifests itself whenever a new landlord or landlady takes over the running of the inn. Much of the goings-on are akin to mischievous poltergeist activity. Indeed, it is claimed that on one occasion two glasses were seen floating above the bar by several witnesses, then they plummeted to the floor and shattered.

Dartmoor Inn, Devon

Devil's Stone Inn, Devon

DEVIL'S STONE INN, SHEBBEAR, DEVON

As you enter the Devil's Stone Inn there is an imposing wooden staircase that greets you, and the bar is to the right with a restaurant to the left. The inn is also reputedly attached to the church by a hidden tunnel. Traditionally a young girl (aged about seven) wearing a white smock is said to haunt this pub, possibly as a result of a man being murdered here in the past. This youngster is also blamed for poltergeist activity that has included pictures falling from walls, taps being turned on, beds being ruffled, lights being turned on and light bulbs blowing, windows being opened, beer taps being turned on and so on. The man was said to have been a fugitive who arrived with his daughter and was later found dead. Some claim that his ghost, complete with grey beard, has also been seen here in the pub. Also, lots of people have heard loud footsteps coming from upstairs when in fact nobody is there and Teacher's whisky once named this as one of the twelve most haunted pubs in the country. A resident chef from a few years ago said he was often possessed by an unnatural feeling of being watched when nobody was around. He spent some time living in room No. 4 and was occasionally awoken by the sounds of someone walking heavily up and down the hallway outside. Whoever it was would walk continuously along the length of the hallway but would periodically stop. This could happen for a long phase of time but there was never anyone there when it was investigated.

A Devon investigation team spent an interesting night here and their medium correctly identified that there had previously been a fire in part of the building as well as picking up on other intriguing information. A séance was held in the bar area and one team member began to be affected by persistent back pain (something he does not usually suffer from). Intriguingly, it transpired that had had been standing on the very spot where one of the locals had fallen off his stool and died.

Dolphin Tavern, Penzance, Cornwall

The Dolphin Inn's proximity to the sea, (it is positioned right across from the entrance to Penzance Harbour), has meant that it has echoed to the reverberant chitchat of the seafaring fraternity for over 500 years, dating back to the sixteenth century; it has acquired a great deal of colourful history. Tunnels and secret rooms have been unearthed in the past, which even contained old oak casks. It is said that the great Elizabethan sailor Sir John Hawkins used it in 1588 as his base to recruit and organize the Cornish fleet that fought the Spanish Armada. Tradition maintains that the first tobacco to be smoked in England wafted among its wooden rafters after a visit from Sir Walter Raleigh. Later, the infamous Judge Jeffreys is reputed to have turned the Dolphin Tavern's dining room into a courtroom and its cellar into a jail when he came for savage retribution

Dolphin Tavern, Penzance, Cornwall

against the Monmouth rebels in 1685, though history doesn't appear to support this idea. In the mid-nineteenth century two separate landlords were fined for two differing reasons. Firstly, the proprietor, William Pascoe, was fined for refusing to billet soldiers at the Dolphin Tavern, and his successor, Mr Patch, found himself hauled up before the authorities for harbouring loose women on the premises. By the early twentieth century, however, the inn had become a respectable drinking place and it was a favoured stopover for the gentry awaiting the ships that would depart from the harbour opposite, bound for the nearby Isles of Scilly.

At least three ghosts are said to reside within the Dolphin Tavern's history-steeped walls and the pub has been featured in many a ghost-themed journal. The most famous of the pub's spooks is a salty old sea captain with a bushy beard who wears a tri-cornered hat, lace ruffles and a magnificent jacket with shiny brass buttons. Successive landlords have come to know him as George and have been happy to allow him to continue his spooky wanders, with several witnesses mistaking him for a costumed staff member. Even today there have been several recent encounters, including one barmaid witnessing him drifting across the bar. Footsteps with a heavy and determined tread are regularly heard from above and some claim this is also down to George.

Another ghost is that of a woman in Victorian dress. Allegedly, she flits across the main bar in front of startled onlookers. One Sunday morning in October 2000 a member of staff was sitting at the bar awaiting the start of the busy lunchtime session, when the ghost suddenly materialised from the wall beside him and drifted across to the opposite wall, where she simply melted into the stonework.

The other phantom is that of a fair-haired young man. Over the years several landlords and landladies have awoken to find him standing by, or even sitting on, the bottom of their beds. No one has ever discovered his identity – he has the annoying habit of simply drifting away the moment anyone speaks to him – but he may well be a young man who fell to his death in the cellar back in the eighteenth century.

A few years ago I received correspondence from a lady who had briefly been employed as a relief manager at the pub. She told me that many unexplainable things had occurred, including doors locking by themselves, sudden temperature drops, the sound of footsteps when nobody was around, banging and crashing noises, mysterious breakages, and people experiencing sensations of panic and oppressive atmospheres.

In February 2004 I led an investigation by the P.R.O. at the Dolphin Tavern. I was very excited to be carrying out an investigation at one of my favourite haunted pubs and it seemed others shared my excitement as we received media coverage from Carlton TV, Pirate FM radio and BBC Radio Cornwall (both radio stations joined us for the investigation) and afterwards we were also featured in the local papers. Once the investigation began we decided to split the team into two groups to avoid cross contamination of evidence. I joined one team to begin investigation in the cellars. Our psychics had soon identified a number of presences, including a cat, a lady in her thirties who died in the seventeenth century and a young boy who had died in the year 1870 after a fall. He had been resident in the property and had particularly strong links to the upstairs section. The team then had the most dramatic experience as two of our team members independently saw a tall, long-haired ghostly figure. At the same time two other team members heard a peculiar noise, and a fifth, and sceptical, team member had a sudden gripping pain in his chest. At this point the EMF meter also gave a reading that was off the scale!

The psychics present identified the long-haired apparition as a man in his fifties who'd died of a heart attack. When he was alive he had worked on a Spanish ship based at Penzance harbour and had been a merchant who exported goods. He had therefore spent most of his time at sea but had been staying at the inn at the time of his death (staying at the inn was something he generally had done when ashore and he loved having a drink here).

When the other group attended the cellar, they also identified a young blonde-haired boy who'd died in an accident from a fall. The group though came up with the date 1872 in relation to this presence. They then picked up on a female who'd died from heart-related problems and a male in his late forties who'd collapsed and died in the seventeenth century. He was described as having a haggard, weather beaten face, broken nose, greasy grey hair and wearing a leather waistcoat. They also discovered that he was a sailor and got the name Bolitho, which is indeed a very familiar local name.

The other group ventured into the kitchen and picked up on a female spirit called Doris, aged fifty-eight, whose presence apparently scared one of the radio presenters into exiting the area. It is believed she may have worked at the pub, employed as what she described as a 'general dogsbody' and although she worked here for seven years had not especially enjoyed her job. Our psychic could see her form and described her as being about 5ft 8in, not especially attractive and wearing a brown headscarf with hair rollers underneath and a grey cardigan. She apparently moves around the kitchen and bar areas as if she is still carrying out her duties and likes to show herself to customers.

In the bar area the team picked up on a male presence from the seventeenth century, a smuggler who had been a bit of a ladies' man and, possibly, had been hung for a crime he had not committed. When asked about whether he was a smuggler, he had apparently replied, 'weren't they all'. He was described as wearing a tricorn hat and black clothes and although he was English his mother had been Portuguese and his father English. He indicated that he has the capacity to move things around.

Overall what impressed me the most about the findings from this investigation was that the two psychics did pick up on very similar information to each other, despite being in separate teams and having no opportunity to compare notes.

Druid's Arms, Stanton Drew, Bristol, Somerset

An easy seven-mile drive from Bristol, near Chew Magna, is a real gem of a place and one of the most interesting and unique of pubs. The Druid's Arms has a group of three large megaliths, which sit in the pub garden and make up just a part of the prehistoric Stanton Drew stone circle complex. Local legend decrees that he could be one of a dozen or so who were turned to stone by the Devil for dancing on a Sunday.

Sightings of a woman sat in the bar have been reported and she has also been seen in the ladies' toilet. The sound of footsteps in the area of the ladies' toilets was picked up by the camcorder of a local paranormal investigator who also heard knocks coming from the fireplace. The landlord says that a picture was once launched off the wall in the lounge in front of six visitors and smashed and that his dog will not enter the room.

Drum & Monkey Inn, Kenn, Somerset

This intriguingly titled pub is a splendid old village inn dating back to the 1720s.

Famously the ghost story centres on Nellie No Change, a unique landlady known for many miles around, whose friendly form apparently returns to make an appearance or two at the inn. She got her name from the fact that whenever she received wealthy looking customers she would take their money with the words 'no change' assuming they could afford to lose a few coppers.

CHAPTER 5

EAST DART HOTEL, POSTBRIDGE, DEVON

This is slap bang in the midst of 'hunting-country' as I was unfortunate enough to find out one day. As for the pub itself? Well, of all things it is a drunken dog that allegedly haunts it. A former landlady was possessed one day by a sudden religious and salubrious zeal and decided to remove all alcohol from the pub, proceeding to pour it into a nearby ditch. The hound in question came along and began to lap it up until falling into a drunken stupor and howling at the moon. This canine wraith is said to continue to repeat this uncanny manifestation to this very day. Imagine that… getting drunk for all eternity!

East Dart Hotel, Postbridge, Devon

East Dart Hotel, Postbridge, Devon

ELIOT ARMS, TREGADILLETT, CORNWALL

The Eliot Arms, formerly known as the Square and Compass Inn, is a fabulous little pub and is really well positioned off the A30 just inside the Cornish border past Launceston. The pub itself dates from the fourteenth century and has an interesting collection of black-beamed, low-ceilinged rooms, packed with antiques and curios. It is believed to have once been a mason's lodge for French prisoners of war, during Napoleonic times.

The main haunting seems to be that of an unseen presence or what is described as a white or grey shadow, with people often getting a sense of being watched. The shape has been witnessed moving through a solid wall and by several people, usually in the dining room, with one person describing the shadow as having a visible shoulder. Other alleged ghosts at the property include a Victorian lady and a young girl. Ghostly female singing has also apparently been heard, along with other strange goings on such as things going missing and then reappearing at a later date.

CHAPTER 6

Farmer's Arms, Woolfardisworthy, Devon

Parts of the building date back to the thirteenth century and recently the landlord discovered a hidden well in the bar that could possibly be Anglo-Saxon. He suggests that there has been a distinct change in atmosphere since the well was opened and strange things have been happening in the building ever since. His wife was thrown off a chair by an invisible force and found herself stroked by an unseen hand when alone in bed; their daughter was scared by the apparition of an old tramp walking past the well and disappearing, as well as a ghostly face in an upstairs room; doors keep opening and closing inexplicably; a member of staff was hit on the head by a glass bowl which flew off a table in the kitchen; on two occasions the kitchen clock flew off the wall, while people looked on in disbelief; and phantom footsteps have been heard.

Mediums who have visited the pub have suggested a murder may have taken place by the well centuries ago, and that the property is also haunted by the ghost of a previous landlord, Roy Chappell, who was there in the 1960s and 1970s and was a bit of a joker.

Ferryhouse Inn, St Budeaux, Plymouth, Devon

The Ferry House Inn is about 300 years old and was the last place for travellers to take sustenance before riding the ferry to Saltash in Cornwall. The inn is named after the ferry which carried passengers and vehicles across the River Tamar and was the main route over until the building of the Tamar Bridge in 1961.

The pub is allegedly haunted by an old woman, a former tenant of the building who has been making appearances for many years. There is also said to be a young girl, whose origins are less clear. Various clientele and landlords have talked about strange sounds, such as footsteps on the stairs, sudden drops in temperature and animals playing up.

Finnygook Inn, Crafthole, Cornwall

The Finnygook is a fifteenth-century coaching inn at Crafthole in the south-east of Cornwall, it was formerly known as the New Inn and is one of the few pubs to take its name from its ghost. In the eighteenth century a notorious smuggler named Silas Finny lived locally. He had a severe disagreement with his fellow law-breakers over the precise details of the proposed landing of a cargo of brandy, lace and tobacco at Whitsand Bay. As a result of this disagreement he revealed to the excise men the details of the landing and made himself absent when the event took place. Accordingly some of the smugglers were arrested and subsequently deported to Botany Bay in Australia where the Governor General was Captain Bligh of *Bounty* fame. Sometime afterwards Finny was murdered at Bligers Well, halfway up the hill between Crafthole and Portwrinkle, as revenge for his betrayal. His gook (a local term for ghost) reputedly haunts the area and some local families who have lived here for many years will not walk the hill between Crafthole and Portwrinkle in the dark hours. Finny has not been seen in the inn that now bears his name for many years. However, there have been some unexplainable incidents that occur from time to time including strange sounds and mischievous activity such as objects being moved and hidden.

First & Last Inn, Sennen, Cornwall

The First & Last Inn is one of the most famous inns in Cornwall, not only because of its location but also because of its notorious reputation. Since the seventeenth century it has been home to both smugglers and ship wreckers. During the peak of the trade at the beginning of the 1800s people of every status were thought to be involved with smuggling. Many valuable goods were smuggled in from France and the smugglers would use secret tunnels to evade government officials.

The ghost tale surrounding the inn involves Annie George (or Treeve), a formidable character who presided over the establishment and most of the smuggling and wrecking operations in the area in the early part of the nineteenth century. There is still a glass-covered well in the inn known as Annie's Well which is visited by many tourists. She made many enemies, especially when, caught by Customs and Excise, she gave king's evidence against some of her fellow smugglers. Her enemies sought the revenge; Annie was murdered. A group of locals are said to have seized her and taken her to nearby Sennen beach. On arrival they staked her out and left her to drown on the incoming tide, before returning her body to be laid out in the upstairs room at the inn. Her ghost is purported to still be in her room at the inn and to have been particualrly restless over the centuries when new people take over the running of the pub. There are many strange tales of cold chills and sightings over the years, and locally people are convinced that the pub is haunted. Naturally, however, this is due in no small part to a great deal of publicity. I myself have been part of filming by two companies recording at the pub for local television, and a few years ago the inn once again featured in the local and national papers. A new landlady and landlord left the pub overnight – apparently petrified after holding an impromptu late night séance at the pub. Another tenant stayed in the infamous room and experienced ice-cold temperatures and the grip of unseen hands, which seemed to be pinning him to the bed, rendering him unable to move. Annie is almost certainly the favourite candidate for ghostly shenanigans and has been described as an elderly lady wearing black.

In October 2005 I visited the First & Last Inn on two consecutive nights with P.R.O. to film for Westcountry TV and then BBC Spotlight. On the second night we also carried out a filmed investigation and split into three separate teams, independently investigating the various areas of the inn, including private areas.

The purpose of the investigation was to correlate the findings and to see if anything picked up corresponded or, indeed, related to the history of the building.

We started our investigation in the lounge area where our dowsing began searching for presences, finding in total two males and two females. The first female presence gave us the letter 'F' as the first letter of her name but was unable to give us any other letters as she claimed that she was unable to read or write. She said that she was happy to communicate with us and claimed that she had made herself known to past and present owners in the attempt to communicate with them and had also moved children's toys. She died at the age of thirty-six in 1525, strangled by a man she knew when alive. She was not married but had a single female child. At this point I recorded some very interesting temperature changes where the presence was located and one of the BBC crew did also feel very cold in that particular area. We were unable to obtain information about the second female presence and one of the male presences seemed unwilling to give us a name at first. However, after perseverance we got the name Dionysius Williams, which seemed an unlikely name to us at the time. Dionysius claimed he used to own the inn in the eighteenth century and gave us a date of 1773 and told us of a brother who died of tuberculosis, who it seems was the other presence in the room.

We then ventured into a bedroom and picked up on two presences: one male and the other a female. The female presence was Jennifer Driker who apparently took her own life in 1885 at the age of thirty-four by drowning herself at a local beach. The team sensed that she walks throughout the house and the surrounding grounds. The male presence was aware of us but a name was unobtainable due to him not having good English skills. What he did give us was the letters F, E, N, H and G. With this information we conducted a night vigil and the BBC crew picked up on some strange light anomalies on night vision camera, though little else of interest occurred.

We then went to another bedroom, which was a child's room. We did hear from one of the other groups that a trigger object, a toy teapot, had strangely moved of its own accord here. This was intriguing in light of what the earlier female presence had claimed. In this room we picked up four presences, though some may have been those previously picked up in other rooms. The first was a female presence, in her thirties who had died in 1786 from cholera. This presence also claimed that the other female in the room was her seven-year-old daughter. At this point the BBC film crew all felt a cold draught sweep across their faces. Two male presences were also sensed but no real information was forthcoming. Another team picked up on a female in this area, who was associated with the building and lived here as the landlady. At the same time one team member saw a shadow walk past. On investigation, however, there was no one there.

After closing time we all headed down into the bar area to finish off the investigation in one big group and found an information board revealing the name Dionysius Williams, which seems to have been a remarkable hit. Also in the bar area was a single presence near the fireplace, a male who gave the name William White and claimed to have been a miner who passed over at the age of fifty-five or fifty-six due to a mining accident in the 1840s. During a refreshment break all of us in the bar area at the time heard footsteps coming from the other end of the room near the pool-table room. We called out to see if it was one of our team or the BBC crew but no one responded. We quickly got up to check and everyone was accounted for. This was very interesting, and we found no explanation for these mysterious footsteps.

In July 2008 I received the following email from a former employee of the pub.

> I had worked at the First and Last Inn in Sennen for approximately six and a half years up until February 2007. I remember your visit just after the new management couple had left after only twenty-four hours, (after the séance).
>
> Although I had felt strange sensations over the period of the six years, I had never actually seen anything until one night, around September 2006, when I was looking after the pub for my manager whilst he was away on holiday. I was staying in the premises along with my husband and my four children.
>
> I had closed the pub down for the night and was sitting in the lounge watching television before going to bed. I left the lounge to go to the toilet and I saw a little girl, stood by the fire escape door at the end of the corridor. At first I thought that it was my youngest daughter, but then suddenly realised that she was still sat in the lounge with the rest of my family. I can still picture the little girl to this day. She was approximately nine or ten years old (maybe a bit younger) with what looked like straight shoulder length fair hair, she was wearing a pale coloured dress that was drawn in tight just under the chest and was about three quarter length to the floor, she had bare feet with no socks or shoes. I remembered that she just looked in my direction and smiled and then slowly disappeared. On my return to the lounge

I was obviously looking either shocked or puzzled as my husband and eldest son asked me what was the matter, I just told them that I thought I had just seen something but must have been imagining it. To this my eldest son replied, 'was it a little girl about (his sister's) age? Because I saw her yesterday by the fire escape when I came back from work but didn't say anything because I thought that you lot would take the mickey'. This convinced me that I was actually privileged enough to see the little girl of The First and Last. My husband has also told me of encounters that he has had in bed, whilst I was in the office cashing up for the night and all the kids were in bed asleep.

Five Bells Inn, Whitchurch Canonicorum, Dorset

The inn is a charming little place and the landlady, Pat Hakins, is very generous and delightful. The building has been used for centuries by travellers on their way to the nearby Church of St Candida and rumour has it that it is haunted by the souls of pilgrims that sought healing from St Wite. The church, popularly known as the Cathedral of the Marshwood Vale, is simply glorious and is dedicated to the little-known saint, St Candida, who was originally called St Wite. In medieval times, the shrine would have been a major pilgrim attraction and, as a result, a major source of revenue for the church. Probably the principal reason for the church being built was to enclose a shrine to St Candida, although there does seem uncertainty about her origins. For 900 years, local legend suggested she was a Saxon Christian woman who was murdered by the Danes after landing at Charmouth, pillaging and killing in the area as they went. Her thirteenth-century shrine is still in the north transept and takes the form of a stone altar-like structure with three openings into which limbs can be placed in the hope of healing. In 1900, when repairs were being undertaken as a result of settlement, a lead-lined casket was found containing the remains of a small woman, who had died aged about forty. The words 'HIC-REQUECT-RLIQE-SCE-WITE' (here rest the remains of St Wite) were found on the lid. The survival of the shrine is remarkable because all were supposed to have been destroyed during the Reformation.

In February 2009 I was invited by my friend Kizzy to assist on an organised charity ghost hunt at the pub. This was an all-night caper, with twenty hardy souls raising money for the Dorset Wildlife Trust. The event had received quite a lot of publicity in the build-up and was featured in a lot of the local Dorset media. The history of haunting at the pub is very low-key and was not available for public scrutiny, suggesting that people would be more likely to have genuine experiences rather than auto-suggestive reactions. After introductions and talks we began the evening with a full group séance in the orchard, which is at the back of the pub. In the past people had reported quite

Five Bells Inn,
Bridport, Dorset

a great deal of peculiar activity here and naturally we hid this information from guests until the end of the night. The main ghost story here is that of a little girl or lady in white who drifts though the orchard but immediately vanishes upon investigation. During our time here the group did detect, through dowsing, a young girl called Mary. Also various members of the group kept describing a shadow and other things moving outside of the circle. While such things could normally be put down to a trick of the eyes or misinterpretation, people did seem to agree on the areas and that it had no obvious explanation. Also there were quite a few people who kept shifting and turning around feeling as if somebody was stood directly behind them. Other people also identified a boy called Adam who indicated that he had been buried in the churchyard. However, on later investigation we could not find any grave with that name, though to be fair many were unreadable.

We then split the group into four smaller groups and it proved to be quite an interesting night. Various people claimed to have smelt old-fashioned pipe smoke in the bar area and yet, of course, smoking is no longer permitted indoors. Others suggested this was more comparable to the smell of wood smoke or burning, and it is a fact that there were two fires here (one in the early twentieth century, leading to the loss of the original thatched roof, and the other just a few years ago). A great many photographs were taken that captured peculiar images. As is usual there were an abundance of orbs but, more interestingly, there was what appeared to be a misty face in one. During communication attempts there were several incidents of personal readings where a family member made contact with a member of the ghost hunting group. Naturally, I would not go into detail here, but the information forthcoming was apparently very accurate.

Fleur de Lys Pub, Norton St Philip, Bath, Somerset

This is a beautiful village pub that dates back to 1584. It is steeped in history and nestled in a setting of great natural beauty.

During the Monmouth Rebellion, supporters of the duke were tried in a courtroom across the road from this pub and then marched across the road, along a passage adjacent to the bar and then into an orchard behind the inn where they were swiftly despatched. It is said that during some executions, a man who had stopped off at the inn for a drink stopped to hold the gate open for the party. Unfortunately he got hustled through and mistaken for a prisoner and ended up being hung. The poor man's ghost is said to haunt the pub, especially an office area. A previous landlord heard rattling chains in the passage and his wife witnessed a shadowy figure. Also a dog that once lived here became so scared he ran from the pub and was tragically run over on the road.

Fox & Goose Inn, Parracombe, Devon

Lying on the edge of the river Heddon this charming and typical Exmoor inn cannot be missed as you enter the village. With early beginnings as a pair of thatched cottages serving the local community, the Fox & Goose now stands as an imposing Victorian building having been rebuilt in 1895 as a modern coaching hotel. It stands as somewhat of a contradiction to the surrounding area, where hundreds of years past remain visible and one of its closest neighbours being an eleventh-century motte and bailey castle. The walls of the pub are decorated with farming and hunting memorabilia and an astonishing collection of local photographs, paintings and other collections. Though no longer offering accommodation it provides good food and service and was recommended by TV chef Rick Stein when it appeared on his programme in 2005. In the past the building was decimated by both fire and flood but survives today as a perfect example of Devon hospitality.

In 1961 the owners of this hostelry described many strange occurrences, including a sense of cold apprehension and feelings of fear in the attic rooms. These feelings developed into more substantial occurrences, and on one occasion the bedclothes were ripped away from the lady sleeping in an attic room bed, with absolutely no explanation. Later a black pigeon was found in the same room and seemed to be a prelude to misfortune. This included poor health, a marriage break-up and general bad luck. They finally left in 1967 and life took a turn for the better. Also a girl who had lived in the pub previously had apparently died in the room from ill health.

In the 1910s the seventy-five-year-old landlord of the hotel, the popular Mr Blackmore,

Fox & Goose Inn, Parracombe, Devon

had a serious accident on the road to Lynton when his horse kicked him in the leg with such force that his limb eventually had to be amputated. However, he continued to get around with great success with the help of an artificial limb before dying in 1922, due to complications after a chill. He had been responsible for rebuilding the place and may, according to legend, still reside here as a ghost.

CHAPTER 7

Garrick's Head, Bath, Somerset

The famous Bath Ghost Walks start from outside this location, built in 1720 as a gambling club for the notorious dandy Beau Nash. The Garrick's Head has an interesting mix of traditional and modern with quirky pink walls, wooden tables and high stools, retro armchairs with chequered cream and black upholstery and floral curtains. Old heavy Victorian silver dishes sit above the fireplace and the dining room's back wall is covered with interestingly shaped mirrors.

A grey lady has been regularly seen here and in the Theatre Royal which is situated next door. People claim she may be the wife of Beau Nash, and she gives off the smell of jasmine perfume. It is said that during his residence a lot of unfortunate incidents occurred including the murder of a lady's lover by a jealous husband and the subsequent suicide of the wife by jumping from the window. This is another location with what appears to be well-attested poltergeist activity, including keys being pinched and turning up in different places, a mallet disappearing after being placed on the floor for a few seconds, a heavy cash register being thrown onto a chair, candles being thrown across the room, a cupboard door shaking violently and a fridge being continually turned off.

George Inn, Combe Batch, Somerset

The George is a majestic sixteenth-century coaching inn that stands right next to St Mary's church. It has recently been refurbished and rumour suggests it was built over a graveyard.

The ghost in this establishment is said to be a black-haired lady dressed in Edwardian-style clothes, including a long black skirt and high-necked blouse. She has long grey hair and has been seen in a bathroom. On one occasion a young man was looking into the mirror there and saw the figure behind him. She has also been seen in the outside corridor walking straight through a closed door and heading into a bedroom. Other incidents have taken place in the bar, with glasses and cups moving and rotating, whilst coinciding with sudden temperature drops. More disturbingly, there have been several reported incidents in a room at the top of the building of people being held down on a bed in what appears to be the classic old hag phenomena, which is when people awake and feel unable to move. It is also often accompanied by the sense of an evil presence. Superstition has highlighted this as an old hag riding on the chest of the victim but in reality it may be linked to the more scientific explanation of sleep paralysis.

George & Pilgrim Hotel, Glastonbury, Somerset

The George & Pilgrim Hotel is steeped with history and situated in the beautiful town of Glastonbury, famous for its tor, abbey and rock festival. Built in the early fifteenth century by Abbot Selwood, the freestone faced hotel has welcomed people for over 500 years as the oldest purpose-built inn within the South West, originally being used to accommodate people visiting the abbey. There are three four-poster bedrooms, one of which is named after Henry VIII who apparently stayed in the hotel during the Dissolution of the Monasteries, fantastic mullioned windows and suits of armour.

One of the principal ghosts is that of a monk, seen in various areas of the hotel but especially in bedrooms in the early hours. Apparently a lady in the 1970s managed to witness the monk for a remarkable fifteen minutes as he sat on the bed where she lay. She apparently felt the sheets and bed move and heard him speak, talking about Queen Elizabeth. He is said to be similar to the caricatured Friar Tuck, a jolly and fat monk in a brown robe and the people have described feelings of cheerfulness and glee when they encounter the fellow. It is claimed he may have committed suicide in a monk's cell, although I am therefore unsure why he'd appear to be jolly and give off such positive vibes.

People have also seen an elegant lady drifting after the monk, which suggests that the monk may have been having an illicit affair – perhaps this may relate to his subsequent suicide? Another story associated with the pub is of a guest who stayed the night in room No. 7. They awoke in the night to the sound of footsteps and saw a bright light, emerging from which was a tall, slim man wearing a suit jacket and smiling.

Other phenomena experienced here includes the smell of cigar smoke, even though nobody can be seen smoking; resident dogs acting peculiarly, with their hackles going up and barking and growling at thin air; and also peculiar blue lights.

Globe Inn, Chagford, Devon

This was a former coaching inn that now incorporates a lounge bar, public bar and a

Globe Inn, Chagford, Devon

function room on the ground floor with a cobbled courtyard outside. The property also has accommodation rooms, an office, meeting room, private games room and owners' accommodation. There is also a separate cottage with three bedrooms, a bathroom, an open-plan kitchen/diner and a lounge. The pub is apparently haunted by the troubled soul of a former chambermaid who worked here in the seventeenth century. Local legend claims she was drowned in a witch-test after a wicked local accused her of being in league with Satan. The test proved her innocence but was little compensation as it apparently failed to save her from death – and eternal ghostly wanderings in the pub.

Grappa Bar, Bath, Somerset

This is now one of the hottest wine bars in Bath, converted from an old pub called the Beehive Inn and positioned in the heart of the Georgian upper town.

The pub was famously haunted by Bunty, a former Victorian serving wench who was seen on numerous occasions, particularly in the hallway and bedrooms, though it is not evident whether the haunting has continued in the new building. Most people described her as being aged about fifty and when seen she just stands there for a while before vanishing. She was described as having curly grey hair and dressed in a neat and tidy blue/grey servant's dress with a white apron, mobcap and shiny, buttoned shoes. Dogs have often been known to bark at thin air, especially just after a human sighting. As well as sightings there are other strange phenomena, including a laundry bin lid being seen to lift and then drop, saucepan lids rattling and being removed and doors – especially to the bar and toilets – opening and closing on their own, and footsteps heard on the stairs. However, the common consensus was that she was a cheerful entity, with some witnesses commenting on her smile and twinkling eyes.

The Gweek Inn, Gweek, Helston, Cornwall

Back in 2004 I was part of a team with the Paranormal Research Organisation who were invited to investigate the Gweek Inn, situated in the village made famous for the National Seal Sanctuary. It was two days before Hallowe'en and we agreed to some filming for Westcountry TV; a few intriguing things occurred.

In the private lounge people had previously seen shadowy figures moving around, something our team was unaware of in advance. Our psychic team identified two presences in the area. Firstly a young girl was acknowledged with the name Jess Owen. She had apparently been thirteen years old when she died from an accident in 1830, having been hit by a dray cart. She had been the landlord's daughter. Also a male presence was found who had died in 1839 at the age of fifty-six. He had been a military man who'd been shot. The second team also identified a male presence in his fifties, though they also found a teenage boy.

In the private bedroom, our psychics identified another female and at the same time we had some very peculiar EMF anomalies on the equipment and strange squeaks on the ultrasound apparatus, appearing to respond in time to questions. When we sent in the second team of independent investigators, they identified a tall man in a suit who had a young daughter and that are both often sighted. He also claimed to the group that he would appear here and later in the bar area and within seconds several people had seen a shadowy form moving along the floor. This was all interesting because we found out later that there had been a great deal of reported activity previously in this room, including poltergeist activity and the sightings of figures.

In the main bar the team found the presence of a man in his late twenties and a little girl aged about eight who suggested she is responsible for moving objects around. Once again we were fascinated to discover that previously reported activity had included the sighting of a little girl and a man.

A male presence was picked up in the restaurant area. He was a tall man aged in his early forties who claimed that he is often seen and likes to surprise people. The second team similarly got a male but added that he had been either a blacksmith or a miner. At this stage it was revealed that he liked to stare through the window and unbeknown to this group a fellow investigator from the other team had indeed seen a figure staring at him earlier, from the same window. The team did appear, yet again, to have obtained reasonably accurate information, as a male figure has been the only thing seen in the restaurant area previously.

CHAPTER 8

Halsetown Inn, Halsetown, St Ives, Cornwall

This is a typical Cornish pub and a bit of a local's secret, situated on the scenic back road between Nancledra and St Ives. With its interesting Regency façade, the Halsetown Inn is described as 'a proper local', serving real beer and real food; it is well worth a stop-off visit.

The pub dates from 1832, has been recently refurbished and has open fires and a fantastic Cornish range. Miners would have frequented the pub in years gone by and the local MP and mine owner James Halse built the pub and village. Eighty granite cottages and the inn were laid out and built by Halse to accommodate his growing workforce of miners. Each house had its own very small plot of land and this was considered enough to encourage the residents to vote for him, as he wished to become the local Member of Parliament. The village was completed in good time for polling day – 11 December 1832.

The Halsetown Inn, Halsetown, St Ives, Cornwall

As for the inn itself? Well, there are rumours that it is haunted and a few years ago I did receive a letter from a gentleman from Australia. He wrote to say 'I was told some years ago, by a reputable source, that he had seen very clearly an apparition of a woman in nineteenth-century dress on the first floor of the Halsetown Inn, just outside of St Ives'. Funnily enough, since then I have been told a similar story from another source entirely. This was a local man who was convinced the pub is haunted and referred to a Victorian woman.

HIGHWAYMAN INN, SOURTON, OKEHAMPTON, DEVON

This has to be the most unique pub I have ever visited, a must see. It is a veritable Aladdin's cave of gothic artefacts and peculiar maritime furnishings, a delight to the eye. Originally built in 1282, the Highwayman Inn has always been used as a public house, though at times it also had the dual purpose of being used as a farm.

It has been claimed to be the South West's most haunted pub and, certainly, a wide array of paranormal activity has been claimed here. This has included the widespread capture of light anomalies and orbs on camera and the reporting of strange atmospheres and peculiar feelings. Other interesting, and perhaps less explainable, incidents are the multiple sightings of a man dressed in green with a feather in his hat. He has been seen on many occasions walking through a wall and most of those who have claimed to

Highwayman Inn, Sourton, Okehampton, Devon

witness him would not have known that this part of the pub used to be the walkway to the stable block. This figure is supposed be a man named Samuel, a Cavalier who died during a battle and apparently cannot leave the inn. There was, in fact, a historic clash at Sourton Cross during the Civil War on 25 April 1963 where the Royalists suffered a defeat. I visited the inn and the surrounding area near to the anniversary but, sadly, had nothing of real interest to report.

Inside the pub is a very eye-catching door, which was claimed from a shipwrecked boat called the *Diana*, where several members of the crew perished. Some have claimed that the sailors' lost souls may now haunt the Galleon Bar, especially the captain, Bill. It is perhaps disappointing that no highwaymen are reported to haunt the pub, though they did apparently frequent the area in the past.

Other ghosts claimed to frequent the Highwayman Inn are a monk and a lady in a mobcap, though the reasons why they haunt the pub are unclear.

Holman Clavel Inn, Culmhead, Taunton, Somerset

This whitewashed inn is said to be about 600 years old and was used as a rest stop for monks heading on pilgrimage to Glastonbury. The name is said to come from when the holmans used to cut holly trees on a nearby hill and enjoy a pint afterwards here by the fire. In later years it was a bailiff's cottage and was said to have witnessed ghostly activity for many years, especially in the 1940s.

The pub was said to house a spirit known as 'Chimbley Charlie', a kind of protective hearth spirit – at times quite mischievous – once thought to reside in many homes. Items such as keys, books, tablecloths, postage stamps and money would disappear only to reappear some time later. Loud noises, such as crashes; heavy furniture being moved around; masonry falling; glass being, mysteriously, broken; footsteps, heard when no one was around; door handles, turning and rattling in doors; and electrical problems were all prevalent.

However, the most consistent phenomena recently is the raucous din of skittles being thrown late at night in the skittle alley, despite the fact that nobody is up and certainly nobody is playing skittles! Most recently the ghost has been claimed to be that of a monk seen in one of the bedrooms. Just possibly, this monk was on his way to pilgrimage at Glastonbury Abbey when he succumbed to the pleasures of the flesh and other sins such as drinking and gaming – especially skittles!

CHAPTER 9

Jamaica Inn, Bolventor, Launceston, Cornwall

Built in 1750, Jamaica Inn was a coaching inn where weary travellers using the turnpike between Launceston and Bodmin would stay after crossing the wild and treacherous moor. Jamaica Inn was remote and isolated in the midst of untamed and rugged countryside so it was an excellent stopping place on the way to Devon and onward. Some of the travellers were a little less respectable than most and used the building to hide away the contraband they had smuggled ashore. In 1778 the inn was extended to include a coach house, stables and a tack room creating the L-shaped main part of the building as it is today.

Jamaica Inn nowadays is well known for its ghosts, with many documented accounts of sightings and paranormal events. There are said to be several ghostly inhabitants

Jamaica Inn, Bolventor, Launceston, Cornwall

who have been seen or heard at the inn. Footsteps have frequently been heard travelling along an upstairs corridor and into one of the accommodation rooms. This is the same bedroom where people have apparently seen a figure in a tricorn hat and long overcoat standing by the door. He is then observed walking past the bed and disappearing through the wardrobe, leaving behind him an icy blast of air. It is also quite possible that the same figure is the one seen downstairs in the Du Maurier restaurant, where he proceeds to walk straight through a thick panelled door. A similar figure has been seen in the courtyard outside, heading towards the inn, and a cloaked man – possibly the same one – has also been observed in the kitchen area, an area that would have once been the site of the stable block. In the same area, strange sounds akin to shouting and talking have been heard and these voices have a very strong Cornish dialect, indeed some have stated that conversations were taking place in the Cornish language, something that is not really spoken today. Other sounds frequently heard outside the inn are those of horses' hoof beats and the rattling of coaches' wheels, trundling across the cobbled courtyard. On fewer occasions this has been followed by a sound like something heavy being unloaded. Another ghostly figure also is seen on misty nights riding on horseback. It is believed to be waiting on some unseen person.

On the 2 August 2000 a peculiar photograph was taken at the inn, believed by many to be a genuine ghostly figure. A man was visiting and decided to take a random photograph of his wife and daughter. When they had the film developed there was an unmistakeable figure standing behind them. Although it is somewhat distorted there appears to be nothing in the vicinity to cause the effect. However, perhaps Jamaica Inn's most infamous story is one that relates to a mysterious man seen sitting on a wall outside the building. He is reputed to be the ghost of man who was murdered many years ago, possibly a sailor and/or smuggler. The unfortunate victim had been drinking in the inn when he was called outside. The next morning his body was discovered on lonely, nearby Bodmin Moor. Apparently the murderer was never found and the crime went unsolved. The ghostly figure is, allegedly, the spitting image of the poor soul who left the pub that night, and after his appearances outside footsteps are then sometimes heard inside the pub. Local legend has it that he is returning to drink his ale, left unfinished on the bar all those years ago.

In September 2004 P.R.O. was given the opportunity to investigate Jamaica Inn, alongside a reporter from the *Independent* newspaper. As we ventured into the notorious Generator Room, which has since being renovated into a reception area, we encountered a skeleton, placed here assumedly by a member of staff for a joke. One of our team then dowsed and picked up on a male, aged fifty-seven, who worked here until his death in 1887. He may have been poisoned somewhere in the building. Another male, a stronger presence, had been a visitor to the building and died in the year 1784. Our dowser discovered that he was apparently not happy for us to be there and was hostile. At this moment the laser thermometer showed a drop in temperature of 5°C and an EMF meter in my pocket (not being touched) suddenly began to make a noise, showing a high reading. At this point a team member filmed a peculiar light anomaly on night vision camera. This was like a long arced light floating down from the ceiling in the area where the presence had been noted. There is supposed to be a presence here of a man who had been hung from the rafters in 1791 – linked to smuggling – who is hostile, so it was certainly an interesting start.

I then led my team to the kitchen and our dowser picked up on three presences, including a mother and daughter who were in the back. The mother had been a barmaid aged seventy-three years old when she had committed suicide and her daughter had died aged seventeen (before her mother). The team identified the surname of both as Fenic. The third presence was in the front kitchen, a male who had died here in the eighteenth century. Unbeknown to our dowser, at the beginning of the evening the inn's receptionist told me that a member of the kitchen staff had seen ghostly figures earlier that evening – a lady with a child in the kitchen. Could this have been the mother and daughter that were picked up on by the team? Very interesting indeed!

We then ventured into the area known as the log store and again began to dowse. There was only one presence here, a male who seemingly did not want us there. He had apparently worked here in this building and been murdered by three men in this room as part of a drunken brawl in the seventeenth century. At this point the laser thermometer read a low 6°c, although it had previously been registering about 12°c.

At about 3-4 am we carried out three separate séances in room No. 6. I was present for the second and third, and they were intriguing, as three team members who do not usually claim to be especially psychic all appeared to be seperately picking up information about a female presence. They all felt as if she was very scared of a man who had treated her very badly and may have committed violence towards her. Most people in the groups for both séances appeared to be very affected by the goings-on and I tried very hard to use my knowledge of psychology to ascertain if this could be put down to mass hysteria. While I cannot completely rule it out, those in the groups did not appear to be displaying classic signs and they were as calm as could be expected. The information picked up in one séance, seemed to then be confirmed during another séance by a separate attendee who hadn't been present for the earlier incidents. He had not communicated with the others in the interval, so it is hard to explain the similarities. As the team elaborated on information about the male presence, they became uncharacteristically angry towards this unseen being, as he had apparently been hitting a young woman. By this point, my own usual rationality and scepticism of such notions had disappeared. I found myself acting completely spontaneously and began verbally confronting this presence and challenging him to explain himself. Then another colleague began to laugh mockingly as if she had been affected by this presence and I

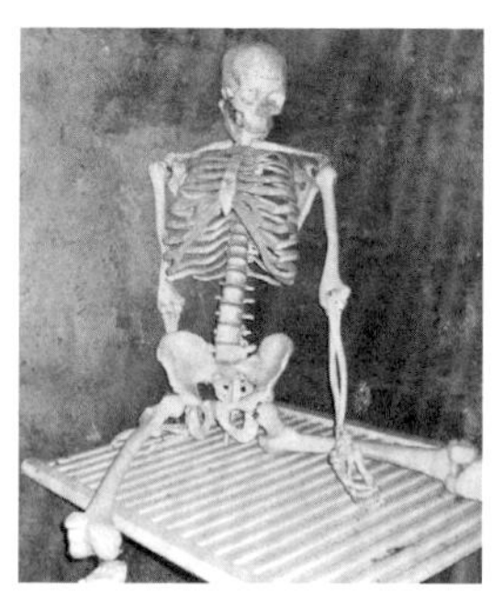

Jamaica Inn, Bolventor, Launceston, Cornwall

found myself losing my cool (this is not like me as I am usually very discerning at such moments). To be honest the whole episode was bizarre and while there was not enough evidence to categorically state that a ghost or presence was in this room, at the time it was increasingly hard not to act as if one was there. I can only say I know the team well enough to know that they are unlikely to have been influenced by any preconceptions or others reactions, so whatever occurred that night was unique. It is also interesting that other researchers in the past have apparently picked up on the presence of a young girl (a maid) who had been killed by an innkeeper. Whether this fits in with our information is difficult to gauge, so again all I can really say is that this was interesting and intriguing but not conclusive!

In February 2007 I paid an eagerly awaited return to Jamaica Inn, organising a public event with Haunting Experiences (www.hauntingexperiences.co.uk) to raise money for charity.

In the first session in the Museum of Smuggling, several of the guests wanted to carry out some glass divination and as a result they discovered a lady called Coedy, who had apparently been murdered by her lover, and a French lady in her thirties called Henrietta. Shortly after this the shadow of a figure was briefly seen but then simply vanished without trace. Various vigils and séances were conducted in this area, and footsteps were heard and several guests reported experiences such as feeling cold draughts and being touched etc.

This time we investigated room No. 4 and many people commented on the corners of the room, describing the feeling as most unwelcome. Then guests in the team picked up information pertaining to a fourteen-year-old male who had died in 1705 and another male who had died in 1640 due to poisoning (interestingly, this does seem consistent with previous findings). A séance was then conducted, with the majority of the group experiencing very strong tingling sensations and cold breezes moving around the circle.

In room No. 5 the team picked up on a female presence called Alice, aged thirty-two and associated with great sadness. One of the female guests stated that she had previously seen this presence in the restaurant area earlier in the evening. Also the presence of a young boy aged three who had died of smallpox was detected, and that of a second male who died in 1926 on the moor. He was Cornish and gave one of the guests a name Erjeald. Two guests mentioned that they saw dark shadows in the corner of the room as we entered, and a séance was carried out with, once again, shadows being seen by a number of guests.

I have now investigated this historic building on a number of occasions and on each visit walked away with a new experience (and struggling to find a rational explanation for it!) Generally, however, it is very difficult to conclude anything definitive about the alleged haunting of the Jamaica Inn, especially the more famous stories. Many of those who talk about the sounds of horses, coaches and voices will have visited after reading the famous novel by Daphne du Maurier and who knows what influence the sub-conscious might have had upon them?

Jolly Sailor Inn, West Looe, Cornwall

The Jolly Sailor Inn is one of the oldest inns in the country and a former haunt of smugglers and pirates alike. Affectionately known as 'the Jolly' by the locals it has been a place of rest and recreation for seafarers and travellers since 1516.

The inn is the site of a famous Cornish legend, which claims that the ghost of a young girl is seen in the form of a white hare. The animal is apparently observed running from the village of Talland and vanishing at the door to the pub. This is said to be the ghost of a suicide victim who only appears as a portent of misfortune, but she is said to be trying to help stem disaster by her appearances. However, in my opinion there is a large chance that this is a story created by smugglers to ward off unwanted attention.

CHAPTER 10

Kings Arms, Buckfastleigh, Devon

This pub was once a coaching hotel and assembly rooms. The building has also been used as a woollen factory, seed merchants and headquarters for the nearby racecourse, and as premises for Kingcombe Sofas. It is believed to be haunted by a classic grey lady ghost, complete with long old-fashioned dress. She frequents an area on the staircase where it is believed she awaits the return of a lover.

Kings Arms, Monkton Farleigh, Bath

The Cluniac Monks founded a priory here in 1125 and the last prior to be in charge ended his reign in 1536. After the Dissolution of the Monasteries under Henry VIII the

Kings Arms, Buckfastleigh, Devon

estate passed to Edward Seymour who built himself and his family a manor house on the site. All that is believed to remain is remnants of the priory church wall, but the spring that supplied the monastery with water still exists today. For many years the estate then passed between the Church and the Crown, with many different dignified tenants. Additions were made to the building in the seventeenth century and again in the eighteenth century. It is believed that it is during this time that the building was first used as a public house serving ale. During more recent renovations, the largest inglenook fireplace in the county was discovered, and when an internal wall was knocked down a key was unearthed which now hangs behind the bar.

There are many stories of haunting surrounding the pub, including a monk who enjoys the odd practical joke with visitors and staff. Another story concerns a woman who can be heard wailing pitifully on the anniversary of her death, which was caused by her runaway coach crashing into the wall of the pub. Apparently, she has also been heard talking to children in a room. A famous event in the history of the Kings Arms is the Miners' Inquiry which was held at the pub and it is one of these miners who is now said to haunt the road between the pub and the mine, tormented by his need for justice. Footsteps like someone wearing heavy boots and a door creaking have been heard coming from upstairs, and the flapping of large wings has been identified in the bar on numerous occasions, moving across the room. There have also been accounts of poltergeist activity, including large objects moving and being thrown around by an unseen force.

KINGSBRIDGE INN, TOTNES, DEVON

Situated at the top of the town on Leechwell Street, this seventeenth-century inn has a long tradition of providing a warm welcome, excellent food and good ale. The bar has a wonderful olde-worlde appearance, with a classic open fire, old wooden beams, brass lamps, an old pump that used to draw waters from Leech Wells and plenty of nooks and crannies. The inn has an intriguing history and was once claimed to have been the regular of liquor smugglers.

The pub has apparently been haunted for a very long time, for as long as anyone can remember. In the seventeenth century, barmaid Mary Brown was apparently seduced by a former landlord and then raped and murdered, legend later claiming that he entombed her body in the walls. Her ghost is apparently only seen by female customers, particularly at the top of some stairs, in the bar, the pump room or the kitchen. She is described as being tall, with dark hair tied in a bun. Some people have described her as being hazy in appearance whereas others have described her as solid. A visiting medium also picked up the presence of a former landlady named Sarah Taylor. Interestingly, records do show

Knightsbridge Inn, Totnes, Devon

a Sarah Taylor as residing here in the 1830s. Also, another previous landlady was seen sitting in a chair (now removed) in the pump room. Other more general experiences at the inn have included the sudden drop of temperatures in various parts of the pub, strong feelings of being watched and dogs who suddenly start to act up, growling at some unseen thing. The nearby Leech Wells are said to be haunted by a white lady and to be full of healing qualities – hence they were a place of pilgrimage for lepers.

King's Head, Cullompton, Devon

Recently reopened under new management, this is a traditional English pub/restaurant, named after Charles II.

It is said that in the past an American airman was killed in a skirmish with a local after a quarrel. The young serviceman was fatally stabbed and his ghost is allegedly seen moving around the pub attired in a full, old-fashioned USAF uniform. A dark atmosphere and feelings of expectancy usually precede his appearance, and he is usually seen near the site where he was supposedly killed.

King William, Bristol

Formerly known as the Jolly Cobbler, this is a traditional pub dating back to 1670 and given a Grade II listing by English Heritage. It is full of history and was originally three houses. Inside you will discover four-seater booths, a real open coal fire, leather sofas and traditional wooden floors.

Several members of staff at this pub, near the city centre of Bristol, have claimed to have heard their names being called out, even though no one else is in the pub with them. Phantom footsteps have also been heard climbing up the rear staircase. In 1998 customers and staff claimed to have heard the spook walking up the back stairs of the historic building and calling out to staff. Landlord John Thompson told the *Bristol Evening Post* at the time:

> I don't believe in ghosts myself but I can't explain what has been going on. Four of us were sat in the bar the other day and it suddenly sounded as if someone one was going up the back bar stairs. We all went out the back and there was no one in sight. Other members of staff also say they have heard voices calling their names when there has been no one around. I don't know of any record of ghosts here, but this building has been a pub since the 1600s, so you never know.

King William, Bristol

CHAPTER 11

Llandoger Trow, Bristol

The Llandoger Trow is a historic pub, dating from 1664 and situated on King Street in Bristol, opposite the famous jazz bar the Old Duke. It was partially destroyed by a bomb during the Second World War, and tradition states that it was Robert Louis Stevenson's inspiration for the Admiral Benbow in *Treasure Island* and for Daniel Defoe's *Robinson Crusoe* after he allegedly met Selkirk here. Other claims to fame are the famous Victorian actors who have drunk here whilst performing at the nearby Theatre Royal. Although the pub now has three cellars there may have been more than this with a network of underground passages for the use of smugglers. The half-timbered work is interesting and characteristic of the buildings of the Tudor and Stuart period, with overhanging eaves, splendid studded twelve-panelled doors and projecting

Llandoger Trow, Bristol

gables. Part of it still retains its ironwork for supporting a lamp, which was necessary in the days before street lighting. There is no doubt that ships' captains of all sorts would have used the Llandoger as their local. The Llandoger Trow is an architectural gem in a visually exciting street of so many historical associations. It stands near the waterfront with which it has had so many links and is indeed a part of Bristol's heritage.

Members of staff have reported unexplainable experiences in the pub and this has included several of them feeling as if someone is sitting on the end of their beds in the staff quarters, cutlery moving off tables in the restaurants and feelings of uneasiness on the staff stairs and cellars, where a medium sensed that a woman who was a Madame in charge of working girls, moves up the stairs to the top floor. She also felt that people have come down the stairs and felt as though they were passing someone but no one had been there. The landlord also reported that allegedly a prostitute was murdered – possibly strangled – on the first floor of the pub.

The ghost of a boy that is frequently heard on the stairs is believed to be that of Pierre, a young crippled boy with a limp who supposedly lived and died at the pub. Apparently his loud footsteps can also be heard in the attic. Two men have also been seen on the pub's CCTV, one sat in the lounge area of the bar, the other in the Jacobean room. Thinking that they were customers in the pub after hours staff set off to ask them to leave, but on entering the room they discovered that whoever was there had disappeared.

Many noises have been heard by staff and customers alike in the old part of the bar area, as well as there being reports that a ghost of a woman is said to haunt the cellars in the Llandoger.

There have been a number of paranormal investigations held at the Llandoger Trow over the years, with at times some fascinating findings. One team of investigators visiting the pub encountered the presence of William, who it appears manifests himself in the cellars as a tall black shape. A security light has also been known to come on at the same time as his appearance and it is commonplace for two or more separate people to describe seeing the same thing at the same time. Also, while they were in the cellars the team heard sounds like stones being dropped on the floor and tapping noises. One investigator saw in their mind's eye the interpretation of a very menacing looking man, possibly a murderer, with dark black eyes and a long sharp thin nose, with a long scar on his face leading from his left eye to his left cheek. She said it was almost as if she was looking through the eyes of a murder victim as he lunged towards her. She then felt as if she was being held down to the ground and strangled and then as though blood was all over the floor.

One of the psychic members of the team was in the main bar when she sensed a woman who she described as a very cheerful lady with dark curly hair tied up. She was standing with her hands on her hips and smiling. She looked a little like a gypsy or wench because she was wearing a white top showing an enormous cleavage.

In the Jacobean Room the psychics of this group sensed that there was a large group of men involved in some kind of devious or unpleasant plot, and they identified a murder whereby a woman had her throat cut by a wicked man.

In the Red Room the psychic saw movement under the tables and felt it was a small animal, maybe a monkey wearing a fez hat and a ruff around his neck.

Also picked up here in the building were a little boy with grey shorts, spotted by one person on the landing of the first floor, an Afghan hound, a very well-dressed man, maybe a ship's captain, looking out of a window and a bald elderly man called Albert wearing a dark suit with either a grey or white hankie in his left pocket. He was sat in the corner and he had an empty pint glass on the table in front of him, which he was looking down at.

LEY ARMS, KENN, EXETER, DEVON

Voted National Village Pub of the Year, the Ley Arms is nestled in the picturesque village of Kenn. This marvellous old thatched thirteenth-century pub, built in 1290, is in a beautiful setting close to Exeter, just off the A38 and next to the River Kenn and was originally built as a home for stone masons working on the local church. The inn was once said to have a tunnel leading to the church and legend had it that in the early 1900s the tunnel collapsed, killing several workers.

Various members of staff have felt uncomfortable in the restaurant area of the bar and the areas leading to the toilets. Although nothing has been seen, a lot of people feel a distinctive presence here and at times the whole area can become atmospheric and doors have been known to open. A paranormal investigation team attributed the area to a female spirit dated to the sixteenth century and several of the female team members felt sick and light headed. Independent people have also smelt fresh pipe smoke in that area.

Ley Arms, Kenn, Exeter, Devon

CHAPTER 12

Manor House Country Inn, Rilla Mill, near Callington

The outside camouflage of the Manor House belies its contemporary interior where all the dining areas have been brought up to date including a lovely bar area popular with locals. Footsteps have been reported here in an upstairs room, alongside sudden drops in temperature.

Minerva Inn, Plymouth, Devon

The Minerva Inn has stood in its current location on Looe Street, Plymouth since 1572 and it is the oldest licensed premises in the historic city of Plymouth. The inn was

Minerva Inn, Plymouth, Devon

originally built as a sea captain's home and later served as a seaman's rest. The inn boasts a Spanish Galleon's mast built within the stairwell, as was the custom at the time. The building has links with Sir Francis Drake, as between 1540 and 1596 he was reputed to have lived no more than 30 metres away. By the late eighteenth century the inn was well defined as a press gang hub where intoxicated men were beaten and dragged to the Parade in Plymouth (located within the Barbican area) through a purpose-built tunnel. The press gang window and the tunnel entrance still survive today. In 1899 the Minerva was sold to the Octagon Brewery of Plymouth and the stained-glass window containing the head of the Roman goddess of wisdom was added.

The inn has a history of haunting, including a screaming man, an Elizabethan lady, several prostitutes and a young girl in Victorian dress.

MOLESWORTH ARMS HOTEL, WADEBRIDGE, CORNWALL

The Molesworth Arms Hotel is a famous sixteenth-century coaching inn that offers a friendly atmosphere, great accommodation and excellent food from its Da Boes Restauraunt. Its name came from the influential Molesworth family, whose crest has been displayed inside the pub.

An old legend claims that every year on New Year's Eve a phantom coach and horses, being driven by a headless coachman, rides up to the courtyard here. However, I do not believe there have been many reported sightings in recent years.

MOUNT PLEASANT INN, DAWLISH, DEVON

The Mount Pleasant Inn is a pub of all sorts, based on the road out of Dawlish Warren to Dawlish. The inn has been in existence since before 1756, and the pub is in a raised position and has an excellent view over the bay of Dawlish Warren. Historically it is rumoured to have strong associations with smuggling, with lanterns shone from the pub's windows as signalling devices.

In the past, poltergeist activity has been reported, including jars and bottles being thrown off shelves, keys being removed from hooks and laid on the floor and a mirror sliding across the floor at a time when dragging noises were also heard. Also, many people have reported experiencing a peculiar atmosphere about the pub itself.

CHAPTER 13

NAVAL & MILITARY INN, TAUNTON, SOMERSET

At the time of writing the pub has been closed, officially for refurbishment. However, an Avon and Somerset Police bulletin stated 'a full review will now take place of the licence at the Naval & Military pub on East Reach after community concerns about problems connected to the venue. Evidence of Class A drug use was found at the premises as well as concerns about anti-social behaviour and breach of licensing regulations. Therefore re-opening is not sure at this time.'

Until that time, however, people have heard angry voices in the pub when nobody is around. Evidently, two men are having a furious row and the atmosphere becomes deeply unpleasant. When the pub was still open, a former landlord actually closed one of the bedrooms, where it is reported that several guests previously left in the night, too scared to stay in the room concerned until the morning.

NAVY INN, PENZANCE, CORNWALL

The Navy Inn is tucked away on a quiet street and has a relaxed and informal pub restaurant with original wooden floors, navy blue and off-white decor, a mixture of Moroccan and high-backed leather chairs and pews. Local artists' work is also on display.

A few years ago I spoke to the then tenants who were convinced that the pub was haunted. A specific picture was frequently found on the floor; it seemed as if this had been gently moved by unseen hands and left without damage on the carpet.

NEW INN, BACKWELL, BRISTOL

The New Inn is one of Backwell's oldest pubs and has a large faithful following of regulars. There's a great little pub garden outside and a good number of seats to park oneself with a pint or two.

A strange man has been seen sitting on a bar stool and footsteps have been heard traversing across a corridor upstairs. Also at times people have experienced being touched by an unseen hand that strokes the back of their necks. There have been reports of objects, including a pair of spectacles and the top of an ice bucket, seemingly moving of their own accord.

New Inn, Coleford, Crediton, Devon

This is a charming thirteenth century, Grade II, thatched pub, lying right in the heart of mid-Devon countryside. It is a cob-style building standing next to a stream. Although the building has been extended and renovated it still contains original fireplaces and beams and is also home to the famous parrot called Captain who likes to chat to visitors.

The pub is yet another hostelry that lays claim to a resident ghostly monk. This monk is called Sebastian and he is rumoured to drift past unsuspecting drinkers in the bar, leaving a freezing breeze in his wake. He was allegedly murdered by robbers whom he came across at the inn and when he threatened to report them for their crime they killed him to prevent it. However, a different version suggests he was having an affair with a buxom young local girl and whilst heading to see her one night managed to trip and fall into the stream, drowning therein. There is also said to be a female ghost at the pub, possibly that of Sebastian's lover. Her presence is usually made known by a waft of flowery perfume but she has also been seen, thus described as an indistinguishable form moving across the vicinity of the bar.

Northmore Arms, Wonson, Devon

After driving around Dartmoor visiting various haunted locations, I decided to head for the Northmore Arms in the village of Wonson. I had heard various stories about the place and so felt the trip through the slender country lanes would be well worth it. After encountering several near misses with the incredibly narrow walls over a bridge, where past paintwork scrapings were all too apparent, I arrived in the small car park and headed towards the pub. I was immediately struck by the solitude and remoteness of this place and felt that the chances of anyone being at the pub were remote. However, within seconds of me leaving my car a local man with a fine looking black Labrador and a stout walking stick, passed me on my journey to the door. I soon learnt more than I expected about this captivating tavern – apparently haunted by a sailor.

My first reaction to the claim that an old-fashioned sailor with a bushy beard haunts the pub was one of incredulity. After all, the pub is many miles from the sea on either coast.

Northmore Arms, Wonson, Devon

However, it transpires that this road was part of the Mariner's Way and sailors leaving one ship at, say, Dartmouth in the south would travel across land to join another ship in the north of Devon. It was easier to travel across land than to take the treacherous route around the coast of Devon and Cornwall. Therefore, the story is perhaps not as unlikely as one would first suspect. Furthermore, it would seem that over a long period of time several unsuspecting visitors have described seeing the same apparition.

CHAPTER 14

Old Black Dog, Uplyme, Lyme Regis, Dorset

The Old Black Dog is currently a delightful bed and breakfast guesthouse, situated on the Devon/Dorset border (the county sign is next to the car park), and the owners, who I had the pleasure of meeting this year during an all-night charity investigation, are positively charming people. The current building was built in 1916 as a public house/hotel. Up until 1916 the Black Dog Inn had occupied the site but had had to be demolished because the building became unsafe. It appears that there has been a Black Dog Inn on the site since the seventeenth century. In the 1970s it was a thriving hotel/pub/restaurant, with people coming from miles around for the good food and hospitality. Sadly, in 1994 the then owners decided to close it and the building was boarded up for some time. When it was finally sold, the new owners undertook a massive refurbishment and changed the name to the Old Black Dog. However, many people still think it is a pub, mainly because it looks and sounds like a pub. The name originates from a famous old local legend about a local man who was regularly haunted by a black dog. The story goes that there was a house nearby and at some stage in the eighteenth century a man residing there became haunted by the ghost of a black dog. In the end the man got so aggravated with witnessing this dog all the time that in a fit of anger he chased it into the attic, brandishing a poker. The dog disappeared through the roof and in his attempts to find the dog the man began to poke the ceiling with the poker, thus disturbing a stash of gold coins, which fell and scattered all over the floor (though some versions of the story suggest they were concealed in a treasure chest). Using this valuable discovery, the man decided to build an inn, which he named after the dog.

In another slightly differing version of the legend, the tale begins at Colway Manor, which was also known as Colewe Heys. Sadly it does not exist anymore, but it would have been a substantial fortified medieval manor. In the seventeenth century the manor was owned by a lonely old man and his only companion was a faithful old black dog. One night as he retired to bed, thieves broke into the house and demanded to be given his hidden valuables. The owner became indignant and refused and so the burglars

Old Black Dog, Uplyme, Lyme Regis, Dorset

became angry and kicked and punched the man to death. Being alone it was some time before anyone became aware of the tragedy and the poor dog was left at the foot of the stairs to pine for his master until he eventually died of starvation.

The manor was destroyed during the Civil War and a farmhouse was built on the remaining part of the mansion, still retaining the large original fireplace and also two large antique seats, which were fixed either side of the alcove. It was there that the new owner would unwind each evening after a long day working on the farm. Then one evening his relaxation was interrupted by the arrival of an eerie black dog, which came to sit on the seat opposite him. The farmer was naturally unnerved but as the visits continued he became accustomed to his new companion's habitual appearances. One day he was talking about the ghostly visitor with a neighbour, who suggested that he should be rid of the beast. The farmer replied, 'Why should I? He is the quietest and frugalest creature about the farm, neither eating, drinking, nor interfering with anyone'. However, one evening while drinking with neighbours, the subject of the dog came up again and his companions began mocking him about the beast. Being somewhat drunk the farmer got angry and he raced off back to his house to confront the black dog. As he entered the property he saw the hound sitting in his accustomed place on the seat and in a rage, grabbed a poker and lunged for the dog. The canine quickly jumped from the seat and fled up the stairs, swiftly followed by the livid farmer. He soon cornered the animal in the attic, but the dog leapt through the ceiling and disappeared. Enraged the farmer struck a hard blow to the ceiling thus breaking some of the plaster and an old box fell to the floor. The farmer opened the box and soon discovered a considerable amount of gold and silver coins dating to the seventeenth century and believed to be the valuables the old man had concealed from the thieves that had broken in long ago. Later, the farmer decided to build a house a mile west of Colway Manor on the Devon and Dorset Border and, with the help of his new-found fortune, converted it into a coaching inn named after his old ghostly companion.

When the dog ceased its haunting of the farmhouse at Lyme Regis, it apparently took to haunting the lane adjacent to the inn known as Haye Lane, nicknamed locally 'Dog Lane'. Sightings of the dog are said to be particularly common at midnight. One encounter with the creature occurred late one evening in 1856 and was highlighted in Richard Chambers' 1869 book *The Book of Days*, which gives detailed descriptions of key historical events, the life and times of people, both great and famous, and long forgotten customs of cultures from every corner of the world. The witnesses were a local couple and the woman described the incident as follows,

> As I was returning to Lyme one night with my husband down Dog Lane, as we reached the middle of it, I saw an animal about the size of a dog meeting us. 'What's that?' I said to my husband. 'What?' he said, 'I see nothing.' I was so frightened I could say no more then, for the animal was within two or three yards of us, and had become as large a young calf, but had the appearance of a black, shaggy dog with fiery eyes, just like the description I had heard of the 'black dog'. He passed close by me, and made the air cold and dank as he passed along. Though I was afraid to speak, I could not help turning round look after him, and I saw him growing bigger and bigger as he went along, till he was as high as the trees by the roadside, and then seeming to swell into a large cloud, he vanished in the air. As soon as I could speak, I asked my husband to look at his watch, and it was five minutes past twelve. My husband said he saw nothing but a vapour or fog coming up from the sea.

Theo Brown also suggested that there was a sighting of the black dog in 1959, when a family saw it on holiday after visiting the Black Dog Inn. The three tourists were walking down Dog Lane when the very large dog suddenly appeared in mid-air and came floating out from a hedge and across their path to the other side. Another sighting involved people sitting in the lane behind the pub and saw the dog appear, describing it as having a 'peculiar melancholy' about it. Others say that the dog is said to look quite normal in the distance, but as it gets nearer to you it becomes enormous, enveloping you and suddenly disappearing.

In March 2009 I paid a visit to the Old Black Dog Hotel to spend the night with a team of intrepid investigators raising money for the Dorset Wildlife Trust and a radio reporter from a local Dorset radio station Wessex FM. At the beginning we took a group of people into the lane and met a local man who said he'd only recently moved to the area but was insistent he'd already had an encounter with the dog one night and that many people had also done so. We decided to carry out a séance and the whole group walked to a side lay-by and formed a circle. Naturally we were not attempting to communicate with a dog but felt such a well-known place that had conjured up such local fear in the past could be a fruitful location for possible paranormal activity. Very quickly, a sensitive member of the group identified the presence of a lady named Margaret who had died in her fifties. She was a happy soul and seemed delighted to communicate with us. She told us that something terrible had happened in the village here, that a boy had been hit by a horse and cart and killed. Separate people picked up on the name of the boy, this being George. We later discovered that the road has changed and that this used to be a very popular route for such carriages, with the tavern being used as a coaching inn.

We then split the group into teams to investigate various areas inside the building and it proved to be a very interesting night. In room No.1 people picked up on a young woman, aged twenty-nine who had been married and lived and worked in the building. She had died from illness and had a child named Agatha. This was interesting because later team members discovered a link with George and that they'd known each other. George had been twelve when he'd been killed in the carriage accident and the date 1840 was suggested. In room No. 2, the main pieces of information that cropped up related to two female spirits. One of these was named as Agatha and the other a thirty-seven-year-old female who'd died in the 1930s. As the information was being collected a member of the team developed a sudden headache and another began to feel sick. In room No. 4 a very interesting story developed about a possible Dutch presence named Henry de Glicck who had died in 1831 at the age of fifty-nine. He had been homosexual and his wife had apparently blackmailed him about it. As a result he did not like women and so would only communicate with the men in the group, particularly a gentleman who was also gay. Indeed, he soon became very emotional as the story was unearthed, and it was intriguing to find that three separate groups all picked up that there was something by the window – this being the place where he most liked to sit.

OLD CHURCH HOUSE INN, TORBRYAN, NEWTON ABBOT, DEVON

This is a historic, partly-thatched fourteenth-century inn and hotel set in one of the most picturesque districts of Devon. The building has incorporated many features from different periods of English history. A Saxon doorway, oak panelling and beams, an admiral's bunk from a Tudor man-of-war, a bread oven and a sundial embedded in the floor can all be found here. The bowling pins hanging in the main bar are from the Elizabethan era, and they are perhaps similar to those used by Sir Francis Drake when he was playing bowls at Plymouth Hoe whilst the Spanish Armada sailed up the channel.

The pub was originally built as a medieval church house and was a common venue for parish feasts, at which church ale was drunk. During the days of coaching, Torbryan was on the main Plymouth stage route and had extensive stabling. By 1938, the church house had declined and was going to be demolished, but, luckily, it was bought and restored by Howell Paine.

The inn claims to have received many letters from customers claiming to have seen ghostly apparitions or heard unexplained sounds. Certainly, for many years there have been incidents of animals playing up, the sound of heavy footsteps treading across the landing late at night, creaking and footsteps on the stairs and sightings of a shrouded figure – believed to be that of an elderly monk – in the bar sat in a chair. Indeed, it is likely that when the building was used as a private house, monks would have stayed here. Many years ago, a man sleeping in the bar one night (the inn being full) woke in the early hours with a feeling of 'something odd'. He looked around the room and saw the seated figure of a monk. As he got up to take a closer look it seemed to dissolve into the wall behind it.

The following is an extract from a letter received from a rather surprised customer when staying in the inn one night;

> I woke up in a hot sweat about 4 o'clock in the morning. I believed someone was standing beside the bed next to me. I looked again to the side of the bed where my husband was sleeping and saw a bald man walk past the side of the bed and disappear.

Another was seen here by a new local policeman who came in one evening to get to know the locals. He asked the landlord who the old man was, only to be told that there was nobody there.

Old Inn, Widecombe in the Moor, Newton Abbot, Devon

The Old Inn, where 'Uncle Tom Cobley and all' had a few ales on their expedition to Widecombe fair on 'Tom Pearce's grey mare' is set in the heart of the beautiful Dartmoor countryside. The inn was built in the fourteenth century and lies right in the centre of the village, opposite the church. The Old Inn retains much of the original stonework and fireplaces and burns real log fires; it is therefore perfect for a cold winter night on Dartmoor.

Old Inn, Widecombe in the Moor, Newton Abbot, Devon

The haunting is said to involve a crying child and a man who walks through an upstairs wall. The crying has been blamed on an unseen child who haunts one of the bedrooms upstairs. Yet when anyone opens the door to enter, the wailing immediately stops. At times it has persisted all night and been heard by countless individuals.

This pub also has the ghost of Old Harry who is seen to walk between the kitchens and the bars. This older gentleman reportedly walks the ground floor of the public house, fading away when he reaches the kitchen. Harry may have been murdered here and his most active time seems to be mid-afternoon.

The inn had a very bad fire in 1977, which resulted in the part of the inn where paranormal activity had been witnessed being extensively rebuilt. Significantly, the landlord said that the ghosts have not been seen or heard since (for twenty years).

OLD ROAD INN, PLYMOUTH, DEVON

Unfortunately this 200-year-old pub has recently closed its doors, which is blamed on the recession and a lack of trade. A helpful ghost, however, apparently haunted the inn; it had a passion for tidying and cleaning. Members of staff have discovered that the bins had been emptied for them, items moved and being replaced and other strange phenomena and things being cleaned; it has to be one of the most useful ghosts there could be!

Old Thatched Inn, Abbotsham, Bideford, Devon

Formerly knows as the New Inn, the Old Thatched Inn is a traditional pub situated just outside of Bideford in the small village of Abbotsham. It has been owned by Leslie Heard, a former farmer, since 1993 and, as its name suggests, the fifteenth-century stone building has a thatched roof. It was originally three stone cottages before being converted into a public house. The interior of this ancient inn is equally charming and full of character as many of the building's original features remain. In the recently refurbished bar and restaurant, gleaming brassware hangs from the walls and there are exposed beams to further compliment the atmosphere.

Not surprisingly, a place this old and steeped in history also has a resident ghost, a former customer who used to meet his loved one at the inn. The extent of strange phenomena extends to disembodied footsteps, objects moving and glasses being shaken. It is said that dogs brought into the pub often react as if they can see a presence invisible to human eyes.

The ghost is believed to be a taxi driver who was carrying out an affair with a local girl here at the pub. The story goes that his car was found at the bottom of the cliff after he had driven over the side. Rumours abounded that he had died under suspicous circumstances, with many believing that a jealous lover or the girl herself may have been involved. However, no charges were ever brought and this may have been nothing more than gossip.

CHAPTER 15

PIG & WHISTLE, LITTLEHEMPSTON, TOTNES, DEVON

This building is about 400 years old, and according to local legend it was used by a French monk from Buckfast Abbey in his unholy affairs with a young farm girl. He carried out his 'biblical' shenanigans in a room which had a secret passage to and from the nearby chapel, which meant he could walk between the two easily and without suspicion. The monk now haunts the property and, in keeping with the story of his relationship with the young girl, is claimed to be a lecherous spirit.

He has become known as brother Freddie and has been seen on several occasions in the past, where the doorway to the passageway would have once been and also in the bar. Some suggest he may be hunchbacked and is always smiling. People have also referred to a strange atmosphere which seems to permeate the building late at night.

PLUME OF FEATHERS, PRINCETOWN, YELVERTON, DARTMOOR, DEVON

This is the oldest building in Princetown, built in 1785, and it is a traditional family-run inn with copper bars, log fires, oil lamps and plenty of atmosphere. It also retains many of its original features, including slate floors, exposed beams and granite walls.

The main phenomenon occurs in a room upstairs. Several people staying for bed and breakfast have reported being woken by somebody trying to pull the sheets from their bed. Other unexplained things occur, including a strange weeping sound and the echo of pacing footsteps. It is believed to be a poor woman whose child died in the past.

On one occasion startled witnesses saw a lady in a brown cloak. The apparition then suddenly disappeared and it is not known who she might have been. Another peculiar story relates to the ladies' toilet where many visitors have felt a frosty draught. Though as Princetown is the highest town in the country – seemingly cold even in the summer – one cannot discount a natural breeze.

Plume of Feathers, Princetown, Yelverton, Dartmoor, Devon

Prince of Wales, Princetown, Devon

This pub, the home of Princetown Brewery, is a welcoming tavern with two open fires and therefore an essential hideaway on one of Dartmoor's infamous windy nights. It has an array of fascinating old photographs of Princetown and it is believed that it is actually haunted by, of all things, a priest. The cleric has previously been seen drifting across the pub. Nobody seems to know why he would be haunting a tavern but one wag suggested he might be after the Holy Spirit.

A former guest some years ago was awoken by a non-existent alarm clock on three consecutive nights at exactly 3.30 a.m. Each time she experienced something strange, including seeing a floating white triangle and hearing music.

Prospect Inn, Exeter, Devon

Positioned on Exeter's Quay and originally called the Fountain, this splendid seventeenth-century pub appeared in the TV programme *The Onedin Line*. There is seating in front of the inn with views over the bustling old warehouses and craft shops. The interior has a nautical theme, the pictures displayed celebrate marine life and there is a striking ship's wheel hanging from the ceiling.

A child supposedly haunts the pub. Described as a little Victorian girl, she makes an appearance mainly at Christmas time. She is seen smiling and clutching her little rag-doll before fading away. Other strange occurrences have been reported here at the pub, including strange rapping noises and spinning beer barrels. These mysterious happenings are believed to be the work of a former landlord who committed suicide and may now haunt the pub.

PUNCHBOWL INN, LANREATH, CORNWALL

The Punch Bowl Inn is a superb hostelry standing on a bend in Lanreath, half a mile off the B3359 between the A390 and the A387 coastal road. Most of the building dates from the seventeenth century, though some bits are much older, and behind the whitewashed exterior thick walls, exposed stone, old beams and panelling create an ambience that's rich in charm and character.

The pub is central to one of Cornwall's most sensational tales relating to a phantom black cockerel. The local parson was having dinner with a curate one night but, unbeknown to him, this man was having a secret affair with his wife. Soon enough their bottle of wine ran dry. The parson ventured into the cellars to get more wine when, tragically, he slipped and fell down the stairs to his death (one version of the legend, however, claims that the curate may have shoved him). From that day on the rector returned to haunt the village, but he did this in the unlikely guise of a black cockerel, attacking anyone he happened to meet. Why a priest would be fated to do this is not clear but he got his comeuppance when he flew into the Punchbowl Inn through a window and was captured in a large earthenware oven. The kitchen maid hastened to shut the oven door and the oven was cemented over and stays that way to this day. It is, therefore, claimed that the vicar's vengeful spirit is trapped in there still.

Right: Prince of Wales, Princetwon
Below: Prospect Inn, Exeter

CHAPTER 16

Queens Head, St Austell, Cornwall

This Grade II listed, seventeenth-century coaching inn is located in the centre of St Austell and has a large, newly-refurbished extensive bar.

In 2006 the Paranormal Research Organisation was invited to send a team to investigate the apparent activity and they came up with some interesting findings.

In a room known as the Truro bedroom, one of the psychic team picked up on two male presences and one female presence. The psychic sensed that they had all lived and worked here in the late 1880s. A story soon emerged, with the use of dowsing rods, that there had been some kind of love triangle. The female, Grace, was fifty-two when she died of natural causes, and she was married to one of the males and they had no children. Her husband, Andrew, and the other male, David, had fought over her, and perhaps over money as well as there was a lot of animosity between the male presences. Intriguingly, a resident guest had previously reported seeing a male and female presence walk out from behind the television in this room.

In another room, known as the Polperro bedroom, dowsing led to information being revealed about a girl, aged about sixteen. The team sensed that she had been Polish. She had worked here and died as the result of a fire, indeed one team member had smelt smoke as she entered the room. According to the information picked up, the fire started accidentally in this room, possibly from a candle. The team also picked up on a male in the bathroom with the name Matthew McConnally whom a psychic felt had been treated badly, possibly whipped. Team members did find the room to be oppressive at this stage and further discovered that he was an Irish lad aged nineteen. A different psychic picked up on a presence named Zachariah Lolmins who had operated here as a smuggler and was murdered by fellow smugglers in 1745. He was Caribbean and buried in an unmarked grave.

In the Falmouth bedroom the team picked up on the presence of Betsy, a former chambermaid who according to reports is often seen moving about the entire hotel.

In the gent's of the pub, the team again used dowsing to reveal one male and one female presence. Both had worked here in 1931 and this area at that time may have been a storeroom. The male, William Penrose, was a landlord and he died aged fifty-three from heart problems. The female presence was his wife and they had three children, two girls and one boy. During a darkness vigil the team all heard distinctive loud taps, a door creaking and sounds of voices murmuring, which appeared to be coming through the wall in response to the team's questions.

On the steps leading into the toilet area an investigator thought they could smell straw and animals. At the same time another investigator saw a shadow and one person commented on having seen and been touched by a cat. Others heard sounds like a meowing cat and fingers snapping, and one investigator reported his ear being tickled.

In the main bar a psychic picked up on a monk named Paul, who she felt was very angry and disgusted with what had been going on in the building (it was later suggested that the site had previously been used as a brothel in the early 1700s). There was also a jolly sailor, possibly called Ivan, described as a tall and stocky chap, dressed in an eighteenth-century uniform complete with tricorn hat who had come back to find his girl. At the very beginning of the evening a male investigator independently saw a tall shadow-like figure with a large stocky build, standing at the back of the room in front of the wall. He described him as wearing a long, dirty-looking grey overcoat, which had a high collar and large lapels and some kind of headwear. He also apparently had below shoulder length, dark grey hair, although the facial features weren't visible.

In the St Ives bedroom, a psychic picked up on two brothers called Douglas and William Trewin who had been fighting over money in the sixteenth century. There was also apparently a strong sense of horses in this area too.

In the cellar, a female spirit, who had died in 1685 and worked here as a prostitute, was identified. In this location a team member also felt their hair being touched by something unseen.

Queens Head, St Austell, Cornwall

CHAPTER 17

REGENT HOTEL, PENZANCE, CORNWALL

This building was once a family residence of the Batterns, a wealthy family whose members provided mayors of Penzance in the early half of the nineteenth century on no less than fifteen occasions. The building was then Perrow's Temperance Hotel but it now has a public bar.

A few years ago I was given a tour by the then manager and he told me about the ghost of a former serving wench who had been seen on a variety of occasions in the downstairs restaurant, especially by members of staff clearing away late at night. The same ghost has also been seen upstairs in the accommodation area and footsteps have been heard from the same vicinity.

Regent Hotel, Penzance, Cornwall

RING O'BELLS, CHAGFORD, DEVON

Reported poltergeist activity seems to abound at this hostelry, a charming pub with a warm welcoming atmosphere. However, the activity seems to be mischievous rather than sinister. On many occasions, noises have been heard coming from the cellars when nobody is down there. The activity seems to become more prevalent when any upheaval occurs, for example when a new landlord moves in or work is being carried out at the pub.

RIVERSIDE INN, BOVEY TRACEY, NEWTON ABBOT, DEVON

The Riverside Hotel nestles in a serene location on the banks of the River Bovey and at one stage it was a working mill. With the river running through the building the inn retains a unique character with many of its original features, including a distinctive open fire, which is marked with the date of 1642. As you enter the building you are drawn to an old oak beam with a sword on display. The sword is reputed to have belonged to William Tracy, one of the knights who took the lead in the slaughter of Thomas Becket, the Archbishop of Canterbury. Allegedly, he later threw his sword into the river Bovey where it was found 300 years later and subsequently displayed in the Riverside Inn.

The unexplained smell of smoke and burning has been remarked upon at the pub, and a man staying here a few years ago was convinced that he saw a figure standing at the foot of his bed. He described this as a man in uniform, who looked towards the window and then simply disappeared.

ROCK INN, HAYTOR VALE, DARTMOOR NATIONAL PARK, NEWTON ABBOT, DEVON

Based on my last visit, this has to be the busiest country pub I have ever seen. I visited on a Saturday afternoon in April and could not believe how many people and cars were present at such a remote inn, nestled beneath the imposing Haytor Rock. It is also interesting to note that, clearly, none of them had been put off by the ghost story attached to this country-style pub and, indeed, had been attracted by the pub's good wine and dine reputation, eye-catching solid stone walls and plenty of little nooks and crannies.

Consistent with many of the remote pubs of Dartmoor, this was originally founded as a coaching inn in the eighteenth century and the tale attached to the pub is associated with this coaching heritage. Approximately 200 years ago, a serving wench named

Rock Inn, Haytor Vale, Dartmoor National Park, Newton Abbot, Devon

Belinda began an affair with a coachman who often visited the village. Unfortunately, unbeknown to Belinda her beloved was already married and when his wife discovered their illicit arrangement she was most displeased. The spouse gained her bloody revenge by murdering Belinda within the confines of the Rock Inn.

For the last two centuries Belinda is believed to have remained residing at the hostelry in phantom form, often providing guests with an unexpected encounter. Several people have been victim to her night-time poltergeist activities. The main focus for this seems to be the pub's electrics, which are constantly playing up. Peculiar noises have also been heard in the upstairs part of the building. Several startled witnesses have even seen Belinda, both in the upper part of the pub and in the area of the stairs. She is described as wearing a grey 'uniform' and is often seen going about her cleaning duties, as if still alive. Her apparition is apparently so lifelike that when an ex-Prime Minister stayed here, one of his bodyguards reputedly shot at poor Belinda, leaving a hole in the ceiling.

ROSE AND CROWN INN, NETHER STOWEY, BRIDGWATER, SOMERSET

The Rose and Crown was originally built as a coaching inn during the sixteenth century and has a very enchanting atmosphere. Unexplained footsteps have often been heard in many different parts of the pub, particularly after closing hours when all the occupiers have been accounted for and nobody else is in the building.

Royal Lion Hotel, Lyme Regis, Dorset

Built in 1601 as a coaching inn, the Royal Lion Hotel has been extensively refurbished, yet still retains much of its original charm. Oak beams, wood panelling and open fires help to create a warm comfortable atmosphere – a stark contrast to claims that a series of executions were once carried out in this building.

Various unexplained phenomena have been reported at this pub, including sudden temperature drops, the sound of slamming doors and ethereal footsteps. Strange mists have also been seen in a corridor here.

Rummer Hotel, Bristol

Undoubtedly one of the oldest pubs in Bristol, situated in the narrow walkway of All Saint's Lane and adjacent to the market, is the Rummer Inn. It has been so-called for over 200 years but was originally called the Greene Lattis because of the building's then exterior furnishings. Parts of the building are said to date back to the thirteenth century, though most of it dates to the late eighteenth century. It has a very interesting history, being one of the area's principal coaching inns and, indeed, Bristol's first.

It was the foremost inn in the area, being in a good central position. Elizabeth I, Charles I and II and William III are all reputed to have stayed here on their civic visits.

Royal Lion Hotel, Lyme Regis, Dorset

During the Civil War it also saw a good deal of action when it was held first by the Cavaliers and then the Roundheads. Indeed, a local historian has claimed that Oliver Cromwell stayed here in 1649 on his way to govern Ireland.

The Rummer was also the base for the launch of the magazine *The Watchman* created by Samuel Taylor Coleridge, poet, critic and philosopher, along with his friend William Wordsworth, one of the founders of the Romantic Movement and best known for his poems *The Rime of the Ancient Mariner* and *Kubla Khan*.

In 1241 the building was owned by the Church of All Saints and thus went through major rebuilding in 1440, paid for by the Church. At this point it was inhabited by a churchwarden, Thomas Abyndon, who later gave his name to the pub hostelry. In 1740 the courtyard of the tavern was purchased and turned into All Saints' Lane, to make access to the planned corn exchange more suitable, and the inn was rebuilt again.

Today, the oldest parts of the pub are the cellars, which would have been under the medieval hostelry. A former landlord claimed that slaves were kept down in the cellar and tells of the strange find of an underground kitchen, fitted out with an old cauldron. The cellars run from here under Corn Street, forming part of the maze of tunnels beneath old Bristol.

The ghost of a man dressed in contemporary clothing has been seen in the cellar, before quickly vanishing, while the ghost of a woman with long dark hair and dressed in white has been reported in the bar. Newspaper reports and first-hand accounts recall strange and spooky happenings in the Rummer, which has seen plenty of poltergeist activity!

Rummer Hotel, Bristol

CHAPTER 18

St Kew Inn, St Kew, Wadebridge, Cornwall

The St Kew Inn is a traditional fifteenth-century village pub, originally built to house the workers of the church next door. Previously used as a smoke house, it is now one of the most beautiful and atmospheric pubs in Cornwall. The excellent reputation of the pub is built on the quiet and relaxed atmosphere, a range of fine beers from wooden barrels and impressive, top quality home-cooked food.

In the 1970s a very grim discovery was made at the St Kew Inn: the 100-year-old skeleton of a young girl. Reasons for her interment were unclear but she was reburied in sacred ground and her burial place covered over. The ghost of the young girl now apparently haunts the location of the grave and most of her appearances have been at times of disturbance or renovation at the inn.

Salamander Inn, Bath, Somerset

You'll find the Salamander just off Queen Square in the heart of the Georgian city of Bath. It sits on a side road in what must be one of the quietest spots in this bustling village-style city. Historically a 'steak and chop house', the premises now consist of a wonderfully simple bar on the ground floor and an impressive supper room complete with galley kitchen upstairs. The pub displays its black woods and orange corridors with well-stocked local ales and ciders, and traditional drawings mounted in frames on the walls. When one walks through this pub one hears the echo of the floorboards and thudding feet among the small wooden tables and experience a traditional and ever-authentic pub atmosphere.

A gentleman from the early twentieth century, described as wearing hob-nailed boots and other period attire, reputedly haunts the pub. This is believed to be the ghost of Arthur Foster, a regular customer here when alive, who is seemingly unable to bring himself to leave, even long after his death. There has been some poltergeist activity at the pub, including glasses, furniture and other objects moving of their own accord. Unexplained heavy footsteps have also been heard here.

Sedgemoor Inn, Westonzoyland, Bridgwater, Somerset

It was near the pub that the Battle of Sedgemoor was fought on 6 July 1685, between the troops of the Catholic James II of England and those of the rebel Duke of Monmouth, illegitimate son of the Protestant Charles II. Monmouth's troops were routed at Sedgemoor and his head was lopped off at the Tower of London.

Claims are that the pub is yet another one of the places haunted by Judge Jeffries, although there have also been sightings of soldiers seen by the nearby church. There is also, apparently, a soldier that haunts the guest rooms and a woman that haunts the bar, regularly throwing pint glasses off one of the tables.

Ship Inn, South Cliff, Mousehole, Cornwall

The Ship Inn's location, overlooking one of Cornwall's most picturesque fishing harbours, is a big attraction – enough to make it one of the county's must-visit pubs. It has all the ambience of a traditional old fisherman's pub with flagstoned floors, low-beamed ceilings, lanterns and open fires. The Ship Inn has had its share of maritime tragedy, as the former landlord was part of the crew of the *Penlee* lifeboat disaster in 1981 (he is remembered by a plaque on the outside wall).

Through many generations the villagers have referred to the ghosts in the many old buildings of Mousehole as the 'Old Ones' and the inn is a place with just such an alleged spook. A strange man reportedly haunts the upper corridor. He was seen by a lady visiting from London in 1970 and apparently stood there against the angle of the wall, before fading away. Outside the pub many people have heard the sound of fishermen heading towards the harbour – without there being a single person in sight! Dogs have also been known to act-up in the vicinity of this pub, cowering, growling and barking at an unseen presence.

Ship Inn, Porthleven, Helston, Cornwall

The Ship Inn is located at the entrance of the most southerly working port in mainland

Ship Inn, Portleven, Helston, Cornwall

Britain and enjoys magnificent coastal views. There is an area for those who prefer to be outdoors in the summer and two inviting log fires for the winter visitors. The Smithy is a separate but ideal family/children's room with its own log fire. The long distance coastal path passes the entrance and the inn is therefore a good place to take a break for some refreshment before continuing the journey. The Ship Inn was built as a fisherman's inn during the eighteenth century, making it one of the oldest buildings in Porthleven. Smuggling is believed to have taken place at this pub, where several secret passageways and tunnels (presumably used for storing and moving contraband) have been discovered.

The Ship Inn has two well-known ghost stories relating to a Mrs Ruberry and a French prisoner of the Napoleonic War. Back in October 2003, I paid a visit to the Ship Inn with a team from the P.R.O. and a reporter and photographer from the *West Briton* newspaper.

Preliminary investigations began with two members of the team attempting to pick up information through dowsing and clairvoyance. Information had been purposely withheld from all members of the team and yet they immediately picked up on the presence of a Frenchman, aged about twenty-five. He had lived here and helped out working in the blacksmiths. There was a strong association between him and boats, which was interesting because the main story attached to the Ship Inn is that of a Napoleonic French prisoner of war, who is believed to have hung himself in the bar, where indeed the presence was picked up. At this stage the team moved into the Smithy, another part of the pub used as a small restaurant and children's room but formerly a blacksmith's many years ago. Our dowsers then independently identified two presences, the first being a female aged seventy-four, named Ethel Baxter, who had died of natural causes. She was attached to a commode that happened to be here on display. Her date of death was given as 16 June 1958. She was a happy presence who had been married with two children, a boy and a girl. The team did not get the name right but the pub is said to be haunted by an older woman, named Mrs Ruberry, though she is normally seen in the bar area. As well as Ethel, the team picked up on a cat that was, naturally enough, in front of the fireplace. It is interesting to note that another well-known and well-attested to story at the pub is that of a ghostly cat. Apparently this feline was a character and used to move freely around all the areas of the pub when it was alive.

The team then ventured into the pub's cellar area and identified the presence of a thirty-five-year-old male named Jacob, of Afro-Caribbean descent who, it seemed, was not especially pleased by our presence in the pub. The team discovered that he had died in an accident on a boat in the nineteenth century. He had seemingly known one of the other spirits (the Frenchman) in life. Some of the team members were disturbed to discover that this presence named Jacob consequently spent the rest of the night following our psychic around. As well as Jacob, a horse was identified, perhaps not surprisingly considering the building's former use.

At this stage the team moved upstairs into an office and found two further presences. The first was a male aged fifty-six and the second a little girl aged nine who had died of tuberculosis in the 1950s. Both of the presences were associated with the property and the girl was described as having blond shoulder-length hair.

Ship Inn, Exeter, Devon

I adore the Ship Inn, a pub located in a back street of Exeter, not too far from the cathedral. It has a strong nautical theme and a largely wooden interior with delightful wooden beams and a stone fireplace. Sir Francis Drake reportedly frequented the pub in the late sixteenth century with other Elizabethan naval officers, such as John Hawkins and Humphrey Gilbert. They would meet in the pub to discuss battle plans, later to be used against the Spanish Armada. At happier times they would drink vast amounts of ale and make merry. Drake apparently loved it here and once wrote 'Next to mine own shippe I do most love that old "Shippe in Exon".'

Suggestions are that Drake and other Elizabethans may still haunt the pub. People have often heard footsteps coming from upstairs when nobody is up there. Alarmingly, it is also rumoured that one cleaner was pushed down a short flight of steps on two separate occasions. Drake apparently took the landlord's son on his final voyage and they both died. The ghost of his mother is said to sometimes be seen at night looking out of an upstairs window, a sad expression etched on her face as she grieves for her lost son!

Ship Inn, Exeter, Devon

I was once here when a lady was having a drink at a table when she got a strong impression (she makes no claims to be psychic) of an old man by a window, wearing a flat cap. In fact she felt he was a farmer called Tom and simply couldn't shake off the impression.

I was also privileged to take part in an all-night investigation here a couple of years ago. Although there was not much to report on that particular occasion, the then landlady said that after we left she had had her leg pulled while sitting in the flat. On one occasion, whilst heading down into the cellar, she also claims to have been poked in the arm by an unseen hand. A customer had also apparently approached her saying they had seen a lady sat at a table on the ground floor – an area where the landlady had also previously seen a figure and where people often report hearing noises like tables and chairs moving around.

Sir Walter Raleigh Inn, East Budleigh, Budleigh Salterton, Devon

Thought to have been built in the fifteenth century, the Sir Walter Raleigh Inn was later named after Sir Walter Raleigh who was born just two miles away at Hayes Barton. The exterior of this thatched property is very picturesque and the interior has many of its original features including the beams.

The illustrious adventurer and courtier Sir Walter Raleigh is said to haunt this hostelry, although the reasons behind the claim are unclear.

Smugglers' Den Inn, Trebellan, Cubert, Newquay, Cornwall

SMUGGLERS' DEN INN, TREBELLAN, CUBERT, NEWQUAY, CORNWALL

A sixteenth-century thatched inn, the Smugglers' Den was originally called Trebellan Farm and was mentioned in the Domesday Book. It was occupied in 1636 by Sir Frances Vivian, and parish records show that members of the Vivian family were still in residence there in the nineteenth century. During times of hardship, the inn became a hideout for local smugglers and wreckers, who forced ships onto the treacherous rocks at nearby Holywell Bay.

On 3 March 2006, P.R.O. investigated this pub and it proved to be a fruitful night. We split into two teams and my team's investigation began in the lower dining room, where dowsing results revealed two male presences and one female. The female had worked here, possibly on the land, and died in 1764 from heart problems. The male presence committed suicide aged thirty-three by walking into the sea at Penhale. This was because his wife had had an affair with his cousin and he thought that one of his children might have been the result of this liaison. Further dowsing revealed that one of the males was, in fact, this cousin, whose name was Edward and who had died in 1782, aged thirty-two. One of the team felt that he had dark hair and was of slim build. At the other end of the room, they picked up on another male and felt his name might have been Samuel. This presence was not happy and plays tricks on the staff and members of the public. He was murdered by having his throat cut at the age of fifty-three, and he knew who his killer was.

The second team independently identified four presences in this same room: three females and two males. The first female died of heart failure, aged thirty-two, in 1230. The name arrived at was Mary Tregenza, and she was felt to be associated with the land and surrounding farms rather than the building itself. The second female had the name

Katie and had died of cholera in 1692, aged twenty-two or twenty-three years. She is connected to the building, worked on the land and died in this area. The third female kept moving around the end of the room and neither dowser could keep track of her long enough to talk to her. However, they did pick up on the male named Henry Simpson and one investigator caught a glimpse of him leaning against the wall near the stairs. He described him as a short balding man in his late thirties, 5ft 7in, weathered features, dark complexion, blue eyes, stubbly, with a scar across his face. He was probably from the eighteenth century according to his attire. One psychic got the impression that he would regularly appear through the wall and then disappear.

Two male presences were also picked up on in the kitchen. The first male was forty-eight years old, named Charles Bentley and had died of natural causes in 1864. He was the owner of the building, perhaps lord of a manor looking after other farms in the area.

In the function room dowsing revealed a female named Beth who had lived in the area. The team identified that she had been married with three children, two boys and a girl. She had died in 1885 from complications after giving birth at the age of thirty-five. Her husband had died a year later from a broken heart and the children's grandmother had subsequently brought up the children. Interestingly, on a number of occasions an investigator felt as though they were being pushed by unseen hands. Through glass divination, the team communicated with a child named Emma. This little girl had died from an accident, hit by something when running into the road. The second team picked up on a female named Elizabeth. They discovered that she had died from lung disease in 1640, aged only twenty-eight. She had been a farmer's wife and had lived locally. A second female presence was detected who, it seems, had died in 1774 aged eighteen, having been beaten to death. A third female ghost named Charlotte was moving around a lot in the window area near the bar. As the team was investigating they saw the curtains in the window near the bar move on their own but were unable to find a draught.

In the main bar there were quite a number of different presences identified, including a female who had committed suicide by jumping from a cliff at Holywell Bay in 1775. This female had died aged forty-five. A male presence who had died as a result of farming accident aged fourteen and who had lived in the area and worked with horses was also discovered in the main bar. Another presence detected is believed to be called Harold and to have died from heart problems. Amazingly, it turned out that this information related to someone well known to the owners and whose ghostly presence, identifiable by cigar smoke and items being moved, was believed to frequent the bar. Also, one of the team saw the apparition of a cat and, indeed, it did transpire that the there had been a cat that had died in the pub.

During a darkness vigil the team all heard footsteps coming from behind the bar and one team member reported that someone or something had touched him on the back. A farmer named Charles Kenige who died of heart failure in 1894, aged sixty-three years and another male called Harold, who'd died of a heart condition in 1974 aged seventy-nine years, were both detected at this point. The team also sensed a presence called Sebastian who died in 1920/30. He used to drink in the building and was a local farmer or landowner, described as having a dark complexion, a sharp pointy nose and a moustache. He likes looking at women and was actually picked up on in the ladies' toilet.

Apparently, female members of staff don't like going into the wine cellars and when the teams went into the area they discovered two possible male presences, one of whom was murdered in 1763 by a single stab wound to the chest, aged thirty-two. He did not know his killer, though he did reveal that he used to steal horses. The second male had committed suicide, aged twenty-four, by jumping from a bridge in Dorset, as he could not live without his sweetheart. During a darkness vigil, a small stocky man was seen, wearing a dark jacket and trousers, and a white shirt. Intriguingly, the other team also picked up on two presences and that one was murdered, though they also added that this murder was committed by the husband of a lady he was having an affair with. They suggested that he had died in 1803, aged twenty-six years, possibly named Edward.

SMUGGLER'S HAUNT, BRIXHAM, DEVON

Set in a truly beautiful Devon coastal town, the Smuggler's Haunt Inn, just a stone's throw away from the harbour, claims to possess a few resident ghosts. The inn has a notorious past history of smuggling. Nowadays, however, it is better known for its ghosts and there have been many documented accounts of sightings and paranormal events here. Guests as well as owners, past and present, have witnessed strange phenomenon here. Indeed according to my colleague Richard Jones the Torquay police force has a whole file relating to the ghostly shenanigans at this 300-year-old inn. In fact, even some of the most sceptical of people have walked away very puzzled as a result of their experiences during their stay at this wonderfully atmospheric hostelry.

In February 2006 we organised a charity event with Haunting Experiences to raise money for the Anthony Nolan Trust. We had an amazing night and returned again in December of the same year. Returning to a location like this was a fantastic opportunity to compare results. Before the investigations began we were able to take a brief tour of the areas of the hotel we would be focusing on for the night. This was invaluable in terms of familiarising ourselves with the layout of the building. Also we were able to gain some further knowledge of previous paranormal activity and thus could indicate to our guests when they were near the mark in terms of any previously reported phenomenon. However, we naturally did not share any information until after teams

Smuggler's Haunt, Brixham, Devon

had investigated the areas concerned and yet it was a very eventful couple of nights for many of our guests.

Room No. 1 is believed to be where a child was placed in the chimney and died. Knocking noises are often heard and guests have frequently captured light anomalies on camera. During the vigils in this room the groups separately picked up, through dowsing, on a male and female presence. Intriguingly one dowser picked up on a teenage girl who claimed she had lived here in the hotel and died of a tragically by falling out of a window. Towards the end of one vigil, everyone present heard what sounded like a knock on the door, as if someone wanted to enter, but nobody was there and everyone was accounted for. Several different people, in different teams and on separate visits, said that that they didn't like the chimney area of this room (this was without any prompting).

In room No. 2 a medium has picked up on the name Agnes and many locals do talk about the ghost of young Aggie who allegedly jumped to her death from an upstairs window some seventy or eighty years ago (the room has now gone and the window would be where the utility room is now). Our group identified a lady named Edith who was possibly old and had visited here on holiday with her husband when alive. She had apparently died within the last year and had often come to Brixham and the hotel before this. The last time she stayed had been over five years ago and her husband had been called Charles.

In room No. 6, a wedding dress has been seen in a cupboard, it is apparently not real but merely an apparition. Through dowsing three presences were picked up: two male and one female. One was a Cornish man in his thirties named Darren who was unmarried and he had also had no children. He was apparently murdered, though not in this room. He had been a free trader and had been killed in the 1900s by a fellow smuggler in an argument over contraband. He was apparently buried at Berry Head. He allegedly moves around and makes noises. At this point a very high EMF reading was found over the bed and it seemed to follow one particular lady around the room. When anybody else took the meter it stopped but when returned to the lady's hands it would begin to fluctuate again. She had no obvious electrical equipment so this was a mystery. Even stranger was that when I joked that she'd 'pulled' and she replied that she already had two men in her life, the readings ceased. The group then carried out a darkness vigil with all the equipment turned off to see if the presence would communicate with us and noises were heard from behind the closed bathroom door. A couple of the group members felt as if they had been touched by something. The group continued to sit quietly, with linked hands, and some people reported feeling sick and light-headed.

During the last part of the evening, several people returned here and a number of people felt touches and tingling as before and then finally a man (a sceptic) began to feel faint and almost passed out. This seemed to be the most interesting room on the second visit too. At first we did not have access as the room was locked, but while passing on route to one of the other rooms in the hotel we heard a radio playing loudly. At first we assumed that it might have been occupied, but the owners confirmed that the room was empty and could not have been accessed. The radio was playing at a very high volume and there was no apparent reason for this sudden occurrence. The alarm had not been set and the radio didn't seem to have any noticeable faults, so for it to turn itself on was very odd indeed. We certainly weren't disappointed when we ventured in either, as many people remarked that they didn't like the areas at the side of the beds and again a female and two male presences were detected in here in the same areas as before. This room felt hostile to many and two separate people reported a feeling is if their leg had been touched. A female guest also saw small flashes of light on the wall and another stated that he found it difficult to breathe.

Lots of peculiar things allegedly happen in room No. 7. Light bulbs blow, television sets are mysteriously turned on despite being unplugged, fire doors open by themselves and the kettle has been played with. The owner was once sat on the chest in this room when she was physically shaken by an unseen force, and guests have seen a ghostly old lady sitting in a rocking chair (no such chair is there now). Unfortunately very little happened during the nights and the entire group felt this room to be calm and welcoming. During a darkness vigil a strange noise was heard by the whole group that sounded like marbles knocking together. On the second visit, a male presence aged sixty-five years was picked up. He was not from this country and he had arrived by boat.

He had died falling down some stairs in the 1630s, and this building was apparently not an inn when he was alive. A second male was picked up who had died aged forty-three but was not connected to any of the other presences in the building and we were unable to obtain his name, as he was unable to read or write. Another guest dowsed and picked up on a total of five presences in this room. A boy aged six was detected who had died from a chest infection and used to live here. He apparently plays in this room and his older sister their parents are also here with him. His parents worked here when they were alive and they all lived in this room between 1918-1929. Beer was served here at this property and people would come to stay as well. The young boy used to run errands with his older sister when they were both alive. During time spent in this area and whilst communicating with the presence of the young boy, one of the female guests stated that she could feel something touching her hand and that she could also feel very intense tingling sensations.

In room No. 9 guests picked up the presence of a female child next to the top right-hand side of bed. Her name was Helen and she was six years old and seemingly very responsive to questions. Intriguingly, when we asked if she could move amongst us to make herself felt, a negative ion detector showed up on a reading; this was very interesting as the ion detector is rarely triggered during investigations.

In room No. 17 a medium had previously picked up on a smuggler who was seen stuffing things into the attic above. This is interesting because there is no attic now and it is a flat roof! This may link with the famous smuggler Bob Elliott who is said to have owned the building in the past (then one of two cottages). He is infamous because of a legend that suggests he evaded capture by customs officers by faking his own death and spiriting his contraband away in his coffin (these antics gave him the nickname 'Resurrection Bob'). Later that day – after his fellow smugglers had rescued him from his grave – he was spotted in the same area by the revenue men, who, as a result, believed they'd seen a ghost! During the vigil one member of the group felt slightly uneasy and very cold and there were indeed some sudden drops in temperature, by a couple of degrees, which were picked up by the laser thermometer. A few draughts were felt and there appeared to be no obvious source for these and they were not consistent. Another member of the group felt that something was touching him whilst he lay on the bed and one lady had an image in her mind's eye of three women standing beside the bed on the right hand side and looking down at a male who was dying in the bed. Just as one group were leaving and had switched the lights back on, the negative ion detector went off the scale and continued to show a high reading for nearly a minute. In the years that I have been investigating using this piece of equipment, this is the first time a reading of this level and length of duration has been recorded. Many believe a change in the ion count within a room, indicates a spirit presence. A very interesting room and some very interesting results too.

The team also picked up on the presence a small girl aged around five or six years old with the initials K. H. Very strange EMF readings were recorded in the place where she had said she was standing, only for them to then completely disappear. In conjunction with this a temperature reading fell from 20°c to 14°c almost instantly. We tried different experiments to try and communicate with her and using night vision and EVP recording we gathered some amazing results. Orbs seemed to appear on command on night vision camera; with some flashing anomalies and at one stage an orb was captured on video camera moving above the bed and this coincided with a 2°c drop in temperature in the same area. I am very sceptical of orbs and yet these did seem to be, dare I say it, almost intelligent. One of our guests caught a very strange EVP of a young girl saying 'one, two, three' at a time they were trying to communicate with what had been previously discovered to be a little girl. One member of the team felt that an area to the right of the bed and across the room was strange and had a peculiar feeling about it that he couldn't shake. A lady picked up on a male presence in the chair and both a man and later a lady in the group did feel odd here. Subsequently, dowsing revealed a man who had been hung in the 1600s.

In the restaurant area a man has previously been seen at a table, usually in a large mirror on the far wall. He is described as in his forties, wearing a cloth cap with a long raincoat, with long hair. In the bar a man has been seen walking through and both pipe smoke and perfume have been smelt. The kitchens are also said to be very active and on one occasion a chef was covered in cream after 'taking the mick' out of the ghost. It has also been noticed that many objects have been mysteriously moved around in the vicinity. During our time here we held a number of separate séances using glass divination. In the first séance the group made contact with a male presence but as one person did not feel comfortable we did not continue. During the second session a spirit presence came forward and stated that they were related to one of the female guests. A number of questions were asked to the spirit presence with a lot of significant movement of the glass. In the third séance we made contact with a male spirit presence but this presence was not willing to answer our questions, so we decided to close the séance. Unfortunately, nothing else of significance occurred.

STAG INN, RACKENFORD, DEVON

This wonderful thatched pub is in the village of Rackenford, about a mile off the main A361 Tiverton to South Molton road with delightful views of the Devon countryside. It's recorded as the oldest public house in Devon, built in 1232 and the cobbled, tunnelled area of the inn is the oldest part. The haunting here is a classic spectral horseman, which assumedly ties in with the pub's notorious links to infamous Highwayman Tom

King, supposed to have frequented the bar in the mid-eighteenth century. The echoes of horses' hoof beats can be heard from both inside and outside the pub and on occasions even from the restaurant area. King was a close associate of fellow highwayman Dick Turpin but was more of an adventurous, charismatic, happy-go-lucky character than him and soon became known as the Gentleman Highwayman. King was eventually shot by accident by Dick Turpin and died of his wounds. According to legend he now haunts this Devon pub.

SWAN INN, ALMONDSBURY, BRISTOL

The Swan Inn is located on the A38 in the upper part of the village, almost opposite an open space known as Almondsbury Tump. It is a traditional pub with a warm and friendly atmosphere.

A friend of mine lived there as a child and stated that a serving wench was murdered in the cellar in the 1700s and another was killed in the small tower. This tower, in fact, no longer exists as the pub had a complete refurbishment in the 1990s. She also told me that one of the servants' rooms at the top of the pub was very cold and their dog would never enter and would instead stand there growling from the doorway. There is also a secret room leading off the servants' staircase. This has been sealed off but the window to the room can still be seen from the outside.

Swan Inn, Almondsbury, Bristol

CHAPTER 19

Tap House, St Ives, Cornwall

There used to be a pub here on the corner with St Andrews Street, called the Tap House (also later called the Globe and possibly the Red Lion). It must have been a fair-sized establishment as it was described as having 'three good parlours, twelve lodging-rooms hung with bells and two beer and wine cellars'. In 1798 the Tap House was described as follows: 'this inn, the situation and accomodation of which are very superior to any other in the town, is commonly used by the gentlemen travelers and others resorting to it and is well calculated to command the whole of that and and extensive business.'

The Tap House was owned by the Edwards family, and it had previously been their family home. Sadly, it burned down in 1898 after having been a dwelling house for a

Tap House, St Ives, Cornwall

few years. One of the Edwards family, Hugh (no, not the news reader!), is said to haunt the pub. One day he was out riding his horse in the nearby countryside when they both fell down a mineshaft and died. He was buried in the family vault at the nearby church with, naturally enough, a suit of clothes on. Years later, the next time the vault was opened; his clothes had disappeared, except for his riding boots which looked as good as new. It was claimed that his spook haunted the Old Tap House pub and heavy footfalls, like someone wearing boots, were often heard at night. Three sharp and loud raps on a bedroom door would then follow this, said to sound just like a riding whip, and, of course, it is claimed that this was the ghost of Hugh Edwards.

Three Crowns, Chagford, Newton Abbot, Devon

This thirteenth-century thatched inn occupies a significant place in the history of Chagford. It has been used as an inn for over a century and has an almost ageless ambience yet is steeped in history. It is magnificent, with distinctive iron-barred mullioned windows, colossal oak beams, a great open fireplace and four-poster bedrooms. The Victorian novelist Charles Kingsley described it as 'a beautiful old mullioned perpendicular inn'. The building itself was once the home of the Whiddon (Whyddon) family who lived in Chagford for numerous centuries and has been visited by a number of well-known persons from history. In February 1643, the Cornish Royalist and court poet Sydney Godolphin is believed to have died a violent death in the hotel's porch after being fatally wounded in a nearby scuffle, such occurrences being not irregular during the Civil War. A Parliamentarian soldier shot him with a musket blast in Chagford, and, as the conflict raged, his dying form was carried here. He collapsed and died on one of the stone benches and was later buried at Okehampton. His luckless ghost is now believed to haunt the inn and surrounding area. Resplendent in Cavalier's uniform and plumed hat, he appears at various times and in different places, including rooms and corridors. He has even been witnessed walking through walls, a sad expression perceptible on his face. At other times he seems to make no visible presence but instead people hear heavy-booted footsteps. Recently a couple from Paignton were staying here when they sensed someone by the bed, a young lady in a blue dress, possibly Mary Whyddon.

Tinners Arms, Zennor, St Ives, Cornwall

This pub is the only such establishment in the beautiful village of Zennor and is a popular watering hole, possibly built in 1271 to house the stonemasons who built the

Tinners Arms, Zennor, St Ives, Cornwall

nearby church. During the First World War, D. H. Lawrence and his German wife Frieda stayed at the Tinners Arms. It is rumoured that they solicited a great deal of suspicion locally before being asked to leave by the local police.

It has been haunted for as long anyone can remember, with many of the previous landlords having heard footsteps above the bar when the area is empty. This happens particularly at night and usually just after closing time.

On one occasion a large dog became absolutely ferocious during a visit to the pub. He began staring at the ceiling and growling and barking. His teeth were bared and the hackles stood up on the back of his neck. The dog then fled out of the pub and ran away. Also glasses and other objects have been found moved around in the bar. It is claimed that the pub is haunted by a poltergeist, which becomes especially active just before a thunderstorm.

TREGUTH INN, HOLLYWELL BAY, NEWQUAY, CORNWALL

This is a beautiful thirteenth-century whitewashed Cornish pub with a thatched roof and is full of real olde worlde character. It was formerly a farmhouse and has a great deal of history.

In the past, widespread paranormal activity has been reported and several dark ghostly figures have apparently been seen. This has included various objects being thrown around the pub. On one occasion a vase full of flowers was launched from

Treguth Inn, Hollywell Bay, Newquay, Cornwall

a shelf with no apparent cause. Particular pictures move around of their own accord and items are discovered mysteriously broken. This type of phenomena has occured particularly when certain types of music has been played in the bar, especially dance tracks; a psychic visiting the pub said that there was a presence dating to the seventeenth century who hated certain types of music. The resident dogs have apparently developed a fear of people dressed in black, especially long coats and this is reported to be because a dark figure is frequently seen, wearing a long cloak in the area near the door. One particular (sober) individual saw a dark shadowy figure moving from the entrance and across the front bar.

In June 2004 I visited the pub with a team from P.R.O. to investigate the reported activity and I must add that because I knew nothing of the pub I did turn up in a long black leather coat. I was worried that the dogs might mistake me for the pub's resident ghost but – fortunately for me – the dogs were kept away from us during the evening.

During a darkness vigil, several members of the team could see a peculiar shadowy form moving along from the entrance door and into the room. It then appeared to move from right to left and backwards and forwards into the room. The investigators did not know this, but this was exactly the area where the figure has been reported previously. As members of the team went forward to investigate closely, the shadow appeared to almost 'back off' from them. It does seem, therefore, that this was almost certainly not a trick of the light or naturally created shadow. This was particularly interesting as it was witnessed by several people and was remarkably consistent with past experiences. Two investigators also indedpendently described the shadow as being like someone wearing a peaked cap. One of our psychics suggested that this was a man who had been murdered, perhaps by stabbing, in that part of the pub. During this period of time several people experienced headaches, tingly feelings, breath on the back of their neck and what was described as a sombre or heavy atmosphere, and one person felt a stabbing feeling in his back. It was felt that the murdered man had staggered towards the window after having been stabbed.

Our psychic team also picked up on several other presences, including two children in an area where we later discovered that people had reported hearing children crying, when no children were around. Indeed, three members of our team also heard the mysterious sound of children crying later on in the investigation. The presence of a farmer was then identified (I must emphasise that the team would not have known that the building had formerly been a farmhouse). His name was identified as David Kerrow and he was of Welsh origin. He had allegedly lived, worked and died here on the land. He died in 1580, unfortunately in his early thitrties, and although he had not been married he had a child. This was the spirit alleged to detest the pub's music, especially a particular dance track and after this was played a number of times to see what might occur, I have to conclude that I agree with his dislike of it! While David's presence was apparently communicating, an EMF meter suddenly gave a high reading, though with the amount of electrics in the pub we cannot ascertain that this was a paranormal occurence.

In the top part of the bar, one of our psychics identified another male presence who was happy and content. He had died in the area due to an accident and claimed to be responsible for a lot of the mischievous things that occur in the bar, including a plant being moved. We did then learn that a plant does sometimes get thrown from a shelf, especially when music is played. However, it is just possible that this is due to vibrational effects.

In the kitchen, one of our psychics picked up on a female presence who had died of natural causes. Her name was Eleanor and she was associated with the land rather than the building. She was alive in the fourteenth century and had had a child who had died at about the age of three. Interestingly, at this point three separate members of the team insisted they had heard a child or baby crying. Needless to say, there was no child in the pub at the time.

TUDOR TAVERN, TAUNTON, SOMERSET

The building, now known as the Tudor Tavern, is acknowledged to be the oldest surviving domestic dwelling in Taunton, with its main structure dating back to the fourteenth century. Beneath the front window on the second floor is a board inscribed 'T.T. 1578 I.T.', these initials can be identified as those of Thomas Trowbridge, a well-known local mercer.

Judge Jeffreys' room here is one of many places in the UK believed to be haunted by the infamous Baron of Wem.

Turks Head, Penzance, Cornwall

This is the oldest pub in the historic harbour town of Penzance and, indeed, one of the oldest pubs in Cornwall. The Turks Head has a unique atmosphere, a place of history that is steeped in intrigue and mystery. As you step inside you are taking a drink in the same place that, some 750 years ago, was frequented by pirates and smugglers who used an underground tunnel system leading from the harbour to the pub, adapted to secretly transport their illegal contraband. Part of this network can still be seen from the pub's courtyard and there have many significant historical discoveries within the pub's walls.

I went to see the landlord and landlady a few years ago and at the time they had been in residence at the pub for over twenty years. During this time they had encountered quite a number of unexplained events, and they believed they were haunted by Penzance's most notorious ghost, Mrs Baines. Many times things have gone missing within the building, particularly items belonging to females, and then turned up later in a different place. They also claimed that when anyone spoke of Mrs Baines a light bulb would suddenly and inexplicably explode. A few years ago a young girl staying in the pub reported witnessing an elderly lady in a room that was unoccupied. Other people had seen her in the area of the downstairs dining room or on the stairs, and a few people have even claimed that they were shoved by unseen hands.

Mrs Baines is an infamous character, appearing in many local ghost stories relating to Penzance's Chapel Street and its historic buildings. Her ghost story first appeared in the writings of William Bottrell at the end of the nineteenth century. Since then numerous authors have written about her, often with disparate ideas about her, and there are a number of locations claiming she haunts the vicinity.

She is said to have lived in a mansion called Baines House in Chapel Street, where a large orchard with an abundance of apples stretched out behind the property. Unfortunately, a lot of locals came to the orchard to steal the apples. Mrs Baines, deeply annoyed, employed her servant Jan to guard over the fruit trees at night to prevent the scrumping. However, she became suspicious of his ability to carry out the task and so one night she went creeping into the orchard to observe him. Jan, as it transpired, was asleep and in dereliction of duty, so a furious Mrs Baines – always reputed to be a cantankerous soul – crept towards him planning on waking him with a shock. Unfortunately, Jan awoke in alarm and in his sleepy and panicked state, believing Mrs Baines to be a robber, fired his blunderbuss and killed her. From that day on her ghost was said to haunt the house and orchard and many people saw the elderly lady around the surrounding area.

Above: Turks Head, Penzance, Cornwall
Right: Two Bridges Hotel, Princetown, Dartmoor, Devon

Two Bridges Hotel, Princetown, Dartmoor, Devon

Situated beside the West Dart River in the very midst of the Dartmoor National Park and named after two picturesque adjacent bridges, the Two Bridges Hotel is indicative of a bygone age of wealth. Built in 1794 as a coaching inn, the building was originally called the Saracen's Head. It only gained its present name in the early 1900s with the modern road being completed in 1931. Guests have frequently smelt old-fashioned perfume and felt a sudden chill in the air in a certain room, and a couple from London recently described having a very scary night at the hotel but unfortunately did not specify exactly what happened.

Tyacks Hotel, Camborne, Cornwall

Originally an eighteenth-century coaching inn, the modern-day Tyacks Hotel is a popular bar and hotel in the main street of Camborne. There is an interesting local story relating to the hotel that apparently happened over fifty years ago. There used to be a particular chemist shop in the main street of Camborne, owned by a certain Mr Beringer. The chemist also worked at that time as a lecturer at nearby Camborne School of Mines. He employed an Irishman called Humphrey whose main tasks involved cleaning duties and running errands around town for Mr Beringer.

Unfortunately Humphrey was something of a heavy drinker and would often frequent the local pubs, alongside his beloved dog, and more often than not he was to be seen in a very inebriated condition. His favourite pub was the Tyacks Hotel and all too frequently he had to be helped home after a session of heavy drinking, so, naturally enough, he soon became a well-known character there. Eventually poor Humphrey became ill – mainly as a result of his years of over-indulgence – and died. Because Humphrey had wasted most of his money on drink, there was no money left to pay for his funeral and it seemed inevitable that Humphrey was heading for a pauper's grave. However, despite his reputation for insobriety Humphrey had been a popular fellow and, kindly, a number of students from the college collected enough money together to pay for a reasonably good send off and his employer, Mr Beringer, generously agreed to look after his dog.

Nearly a week went by after the funeral and one day a few of the students agreed to do an errand for Mr Beringer and took along the dog, heading for the chemist's shop. One of them went inside, while the rest stayed outside with the dog. After a few seconds they saw a man heading towards them who appeared to be very familiar, but as he had his head down they did not see him fully enough to recognise who it was. All of a sudden the normally quiet pooch let out an excited yelp and tore away to run after the man who had strolled past. The man presumably heard the dog and thus turned in the direction of the students. To the students' utter horror they realised that the man was actually Humphrey, dressed in his familiar scruffy clothes, sporting a stubbly complexion and familiar friendly smile. The dog had almost reached him and was bounding along wagging his tail. At this point the man turned and walked into the Tyacks Hotel, quickly followed by the dog. Naturally, the students took chase and ran into the hotel themselves, looking for the dog, which they soon found. However, there was no sign of the man, and when they enquired with the barman he informed them that the dog had entered alone, looking excited but definitely unaccompanied. It would seem that there was simply no way that the man could have disappeared naturally, without having been seen. Humphrey had apparently returned from death, heading into his favourite drinking location followed by the companion who knew him best, his loyal canine friend.

CHAPTER 20

Volunteer Inn, Lyme Regis, Dorset

This is a small pub with a cosy traditional atmosphere, sited on the main street of Lyme Regis. According to Richard Fox who runs local ghost tours the pub is very haunted indeed. On the night of 1 January 2000 a lady who stayed overnight in the inn reported a very strange experience indeed. In the early hours of the morning she was standing at the bar watching the staff clear up after the New Year celebrations, when suddenly the atmosphere went cold and a shiver ran through her spine. She turned around to find three men dressed in large floppy felt hats. She described them as dressed colourfully in Musketeer-style clothing with broad belts and buckles and drinking from pewter tankards. Locals have for many years claimed that the building is haunted, and a previous landlord certainly had an interesting tale to tell. Allegedly, one of the former barmen saw shadows coming down the stairs but on investigation found that there was no one there!

Volunteer Inn, Lyme Regis, Dorset

CHAPTER 21

The Wagon & Horses, Peasedown St John, Bath

Described as a 'gurt barn of a place', frequented by locals and specialising in cider, it is apparently haunted by a man in a black hat who is a mischievous spook. The residing ghost likes to make a nuisance of himself, especially in the early hours of the morning and is especially active when new people move into the property. Some of the paranormal activity that has occurred has included objects being thrown around, such as beer barrels and an umbrella. Items are often going missing and taps interfered with on barrels of beer.

Waterman's Arms, Ashprington, Totnes, Devon

This is a typical seventeenth-century inn set in an area of outstanding natural beauty at the bottom of a steep valley next to Bow Creek and bridge. The area was recorded in the Domesday Book, and the inn has formerly been used as a smithy, a brew house, petrol station, a prison and a haunt for the feared press gangs.

It is rumoured that the pub is haunted by a sad looking lady called Emily, who was a former serving wench. She is witnessed drifting along and sporting a set of keys, which are heard rattling at her side before she vanishes. As the pub was a former prison one has to wonder whether, as she is holding keys, there is a link between her apparition and this period in the pub's history.

Well House Pub, Exeter, Devon

In the cellar at the Well House Pub lies the skeleton of either someone who committed suicide or a plague victim. In 2001 an academic from Exeter University claimed that this

Well House Pub, Exeter, Devon

skeleton was part male and part female and some suggested it could be the remains of a monk and a nun from Cathedral Close. There is also a remarkable Roman well in the cellar and it is this that gives the pub its name. There is often a strange atmosphere in the cellar and a very warm sensation, strange in itself for a cellar.

The adjacent Royal Clarence Hotel was once the town house of the great Sir Walter Raleigh, though to my knowledge – perhaps somewhat surprisingly – no claims have been made that his ghost now haunts the building. It is rumoured that a man came to visit Raleigh to ask for his help as he'd had an argument with his friend, a Dutch sea captain. The seaman had tried to make up with him but he had died before he could do so and had since been relentlessly haunting his chum. It is claimed that Raleigh blew smoke at the ghost and ever since this spook has haunted the building where it is often heard coughing, presumably due to the blown smoke! Also, the Duchess of Clarence lived here and would often sit in a window watching for the return of her husband, who later became William IV. Some claim her figure is still seen in a window at the front of the pub.

WELLINGTON HOTEL, BOSCASTLE, CORNWALL

This is one of my favourite Cornish hotels and one that I have had the pleasure of investigating overnight on three separate occasions, with intriguing results. The Wellington Hotel dates back to the sixteenth century, built as a coaching inn. It was extended in the 1860s and was originally called Bos Castle Hotel, but it was renamed

Wellington Hotel, Boscastle, Cornwall

the Wellington in 1852, after the late Duke of Wellington. A number of famous people have stayed at the hotel including Edward VII; Thomas Hardy, the novelist; and Sir Henry Irving, the first actor to be knighted. It unfortunately suffered extensive damage as part of the infamous Boscastle floods but is now back to its former majestic glory.

In the past, I was in communication with the former owner Victor Tobutt who used to keep me informed of any ghostly goings-on. Paranormal activity is said to be widespread at the Wellington Hotel and has been reported for many years.

Traditionally, the hotel has a few main ghosts, and one of these is a man dressed in eighteenth-century coachman's attire who has been seen in the entrance foyer. Various members of staff and a former owner have described him in detail. Some years ago Victor Tobutt was working at the reception desk when this figure drifted silently past him. Looking up, he was surprised to see that the man wore leather gaiters and boots, a frock coat and a frilled shirt – such as might have been worn by an eighteenth-century coachman – and his hair was tied back in the old-fashioned ponytail style. 'There was nothing insubstantial about him,' Victor said, 'he looked remarkably solid.' To his shock, the apparition disappeared through the wall. Alarmingly, when he began to describe what he had seen to one of his employees, the man completed the description for him. Apparently he too had seen the ghostly visitor on more than one occasion.

Several other ghosts have been spotted at the hotel. A former employee, retired policeman Bill Searle, twice witnessed a misty shape wearing a cloak drift across the landing and disappear through the wall of a guest room. The apparition of a young girl has been reported on several occasions, passing through windows and doors. This is thought to be the spirit of a young girl who, cheated in love, flung herself in despair from the ramparts of the hotel's tower. An elderly woman is reportedly seen in rooms No. 9 and No. 10. She is seen drifting through the doors or sitting on the end of a bed. And finally, a murdered man is said to haunt another part of the building; several of the staff and customers have witnessed a dark shape float down the stairs and disappear into the cellar late at night.

A well-known author of the paranormal staying at the hotel reported his small dog pursuing some sort of 'animal friendly' apparition. The writer didn't see the figure himself, but his wife saw it, as did the dog, which followed it wagging its tail! The crew of *Most Haunted* also visited the Wellington Hotel and claimed a lot of ghostly goings-on, including purported evidence of poltergeist activity and many spirit lights. Also they claimed that the ghost of Thomas Hardy and his wife are said to haunt this old coaching inn, where the crew claimed to have captured a ghostly shape on camera in nearby haunted woods and filmed a lamp that moved on its own.

A few years ago the former owner contacted me with a story about a video recording reportedly showing a ghostly figure in one of the rooms but, unfortunately, I never got the chance to see this in full! Also, friends of mine have stayed here in the past and picked up some very strange equipment failure such as battery drainage and video malfunctioning.

My first investigation here was in December 2005 with the P.R.O. I was delighted to finally get the opportunity to investigate the Wellington Hotel, and it was very much third time lucky! Several years ago I was due to investigate the building with the Ghost Research Foundation and it was called off at the last minute. Then the terrible floods occurred preventing P.R.O.'s investigation the previous October. But finally it happened, and it turned out to be a great investigation for many reasons. (I have also been back since for two further all-night visits with Haunting Experiences.)

We arrived, booked in and then sat down to a sumptuous and first-class meal. After viewing the relevant areas and organising a schedule, a briefing was given and people were allocated their roles, placed into teams and given equipment to use.

In room No. 4 the team picked up on the energy of a male who had been a traveller in the seventeenth century and had often stayed here. They felt that he was not malevolent in any way and that people staying in this room may have seen him. Indeed, the team member sleeping in that room felt as if the bedclothes were being tugged slightly, and another saw blue light, followed by a shadow coming from the room when she retired to bed.

Dowsing in room No. 7 revealed a female who'd died from natural causes. She had been a housekeeper and the team thought she might have shown herself to people staying in this room previously. Interestingly, one team member reported being touched by an unseen hand several times in this room.

In room No. 9 we picked up on two presences, the first was Joanne Jimmson who'd died in 1774. She was married with two children and had worked on the land and in a mill, as had her children. We also found a male aged thirty-five who had died in 1486. He was associated with the land rather than the building and may have been a fisherman. The team picked up that he had died in the sea but as he could not read or write communication was difficult. Another team picked up on a chambermaid in this room. They discovered that she was aged sixty-six and had died of natural causes. One investigator briefly saw the back of the head of a blond female in the cupboard. Significantly, another investigator was drawn to the portrait of a lady when dowsing, and believed that the blonde female sensed in the cupboard was indeed the female in the portrait. She had lived here and died from tuberculosis at the age of thirty-five.

The most famously haunted of the hotel's rooms is No. 10. Allegedly, it was used as a mortuary, storing bodies before taking them up Coffin Way (the track leading up the side of the valley from the beer garden). A very large piece of slate was found stashed in the attic above room No. 10, which can still be seen in its new guise as a picnic table. The only obvious use for such an expensive and perfectly shaped piece of slate would be as a mortuary slab. The dowser felt that there was one female maid and two males in the room, and he also had a feeling that 'dodgy deals' had taken place in there. Overall, however, it was quiet during P.R.O.'s visit.

In contrast, when I returned with Haunting Experiences there was much more drama, with some startlingly similar dowsing results across the teams. The same points in the room were identified, namely the middle of the room, the left-hand bed (facing into the room) and inside the doorway by the step up in the floor level. As well as being identified and tracked with dowsing, several felt tingling sensations and felt that a presence was close by. One guest spent some time in here on his own and left abruptly because he had heard sighing and had cold air on his neck. This time the presences identified included an eight-year-old girl called Grace, a fisherman aged thirty-two, a female from 1584 and another male presence who seemed to have an unpleasant character. Overall, the group felt that the most active presence was a female and in the past has made her self-known in many ways to a number of guests and staff. I slept in this room after the H.E. investigation but have nothing unusual to report.

After this we went to room No. 11 and picked up on two presences. This time we found a girl aged fifteen who had died in 1684 of an unknown disease. The second presence was interesting because it was a male doctor who had died in 1775 aged thirty-five. It seemed that he was a malevolent character who apparently killed somebody and was hung at Bodmin Gaol (unfortunately my research shows that the jail's execution records only date from 1785). On entering the room our dowser picked up on two presences, the first being a female called Heather Morrison. She had died in 1873 at the age of fifty-three from heart related problems. The second presence was a smuggler aged forty-five who had died in 1675 in an accident involving a weapon (a musket).

He died about a week after the accident and would be seen as a man in a tri-corne hat and cloak. Our psychic then revealed that the presence wore a dark brown cloak, black breeches and big boots up to his knee with buckles on. He had been trying to shoot a revenue officer to escape, and the gun went off in his face.

After a break we went to room No. 14, known as the Thomas Hardy Room, which was of particular interest to myself, as I would be sleeping here later. On entering the room the dowser picked up on six presences. The first, a female presence picked up, was apparently unaware that she had passed. So as not to 'upset' her we left her alone. The second presence had died in 1685 of cholera and at the age of twenty-six. The third was murdered, aged forty-four, in 1743, though he had not known his killer. I must confess that at this moment I was developing a niggling headache and was a little surprised when our dowser revealed that the presence had been beaten around the head. Of course, my headache may well have been because I was tired and in the midst of some strong lighting equipment but others found it to be more than coincidence. The man had been a smuggler, killed for his brandy contraband. The fourth presence was a man in spirit visitation who had died in 1594 of tuberculosis. Interestingly, at this point in the investigation one of my colleagues felt a strange tickling sensation on his face. The fifth presence was a man aged thirty-three who had died in 1775. He had apparently been stabbed in the back whilst on the road near the building. The final presence was Thomas Hardy, though we all felt this to be too obvious and so did not pursue for further information. However, at this juncture one of my fellow investigators began to smell perfume and kept suggesting the name Emily or Emma. I did immediately think about the possibility that this could be related to Hardy's first wife Emma Gifford, a Cornish girl who Hardy had met when he was working as an architect just outside of Boscastle. My colleague swore he knew nothing about Hardy but I guess it is possible that he had picked the information up subconsciously on a previous occasion.

Next, we decided to carry out a darkness vigil. At one stage during the vigil I felt a strange 'tickling' sensation on my left hand. A few moments later another member of the team experienced the same sensation, and yet another felt heat (like a hot pin) on his right arm. Later on I stayed in this room and slept perfectly soundly. However, one thing to note is that when I retired to bed I briefly watched some television and after I turned it off I placed the remote control on the arm of the chair; in the morning it was on the other side of the room. The door had been locked all night and I was alone in the room. I could put this down to absent-mindedness but on reading another team's report after our visit (in which something similar had been experienced) it did make me wonder.

Another of the investigation groups identified two female presences and a male. The male seemed to be moving round the room but would not respond to any questions. There was a female who'd died of natural causes in 1842 named Lillian and at this stage two investigators noticed a dark shadow moving near the bathroom door. At the same time the team noticed that the TV remote, which had previously been on top of the TV had fallen to the floor; yet no person was nearby at the time.

On returning here with Haunting Experiences several presences were identified. These included a female, sixty-six, called Kate; a fifteenth-century male presence named Charles wearing long boots, a feather in his hat and dark clothing; a dog, perhaps a beagle; and a male named Francis, who had died in 1972, aged seventy-six. At the same time the EMF meter showed a very strong reading.

Dowsing in room No. 15 revealed a little girl, possibly six years old, a date of 1870-91 was given. Tragically, she had been kicked to death, and she appeared to know her attacker, who'd lived in Boscastle; this sad little girl seemed to have been the subject of bullying by other children. One investigator reported that it felt as if the little girl had tried to hold her hand.

In room No. 16 the dowser picked up on a male soldier who died in 1812 when he was around forty-three years old. His name was Reginald Leisson and he had been a guest at the hotel; he was a sir and a colonel in the army. He was married and when asked whether he had children he said 'sort of'! He died in a battle in Africa and comes back to the hotel because he had stayed there and he likes it. A second group separately revealed a male called Harry who was married but had no children. He had worked in the air crew of the famous Dam Buster team and had been shot down over Germany. He knew Guy Gibson and appears to have stayed here during his lifetime.

Dowsing revealed two male presences in room No. 21, including Harry, who worked here when it was a coaching inn – possibly with horses – and died aged fifty-seven from natural causes. He moves about and shows himself to people. The second male gave the name Edward and claimed to be a member of the royal family, and it is interesting to note that Edward VII apparently stayed at the hotel in the nineteenth century.

In room No. 23 our team dowser picked up on three presences. Firstly there was a male who'd died in 1873 but in attempts to elicit further information our dowser could only spell out 'C, E, L, H' and then 'C, E, H'. When asked, the presence stated he could not read or write – perhaps he was just playing games with us? We did manage, however, to establish that he had died of tuberculosis in this room. The second presence had died in 1845, murdered by having his throat cut with a knife. It appears that this happened in the building and on this floor (though not in this room). At this point one of our team heard a door shutting outside in the corridor but when we checked there appeared to be nobody there. The same investigator began to feel a constriction in his throat. This presence was apparently killed because he had murdered a woman – he felt she had deserved it. We then received the name Geoffrey Higmon. The third presence was also a male who had been aged twenty-four when he died in 1885. It was suggested that he worked as a butler and had lived here.

We then went on to investigate room No. 21 and again discovered three reported presences. The first was a young girl called Gilly who was aged eight and who had died in 1735 of pneumonia. Oddly, as we were gathering this information one person in the team heard a strange high-pitched sound. Then second presence was a male named Nathan who had died in 1825 at the age of thirty-six due to heart problems. The third presence was also male and a friend of Nathan's called John. He claimed to have died here in a fire of 1835, though in a different room. At this point in the investigation, two team members independently reported feeling a tingling sensation. Interestingly, one team member saw a shadowy hunchbacked shape move at the same time as someone else sensed a movement. At this point another presence entered the room. She had died in 1764 of childbirth when aged just twenty-six. Just as the team discovered this information the battery in a torch inexplicably drained.

Another team's dowser picked up on three children in this room, a boy who was only four and two girls who were aged eight and twelve years old. This had been their playroom or nursery, and sadly all three, who were brothers and sisters, died at once in 1843 of cholera. Their names were Edward, Rebecca and Emma, and their mother had lived and worked in the hotel.

White Hart, Hayle, Cornwall

The White Hart Hotel is a Grade II listed building and stands proudly in the centre of this historic town, in Foundry Square. The Harvey family, of great fame in the town, owned the building and ran it as a hotel as early as 1838. Henry, the famed shipyard and foundry owner, built it for his sister Jane. Richard Trevithick, the famous local inventor of the high-pressure steam engine, was married to a former manager of the hotel.

Today, the White Hart remains a central part of Hayle's history and a perfect base for touring historic west Cornwall. The hotel has been extensively refurbished and careful renovations have kept the classical edifice intact, maintaining the elegance and charm of its Victorian design. The White Hart's gallery restaurant is lavishly decorated with a number of fine paintings and the hotel's large collection of portraits help maintain the ambience of this historic hotel. Today it serves as a twenty-five room hotel with a bar and restaurant, aptly called Harvey's. Ghost stories abound – especially about room No. 9 – but the details are notoriously tricky to pin down.

White Hart, Exeter, Devon

The White Hart is one of Exeter's oldest hotels and is located within the old city wall, near to where South Gate stood. It is a fifteenth-century inn though most of it now

White Hart, Hayle, Cornwall

actually dates from the 1970s. It is thought it was originally a resting place for monks during their travels and later became a coaching inn. Interesting features include the fifteenth-century wine room and an old stone fireplace.

One of the ghosts said to haunt this place is the infamous hanging judge, Jeffreys. In truth, his ghoulish perambulations must be exhausting as he allegedly haunts almost as many places as Anne Boleyn. Nevertheless, he is certainly known to have held court in Devon and indeed in Exeter at the Guildhall. Witnesses have also spied a young woman dressed in a long cloak here, and she apparently appears at the front of the building. A child's face has also been seen, said to appear in one of the bar's windows.

At the rear is the courtyard well and, allegedly, many years ago a horrible smell began emanating. A young man was reputedly sent down to investigate and never returned, so another went and the same thing happened; apparently ghostly cries for help have been heard coming from the well ever since.

My wife and I stayed a night at the White Hart Hotel a few years ago and I specifically asked if we could stay in a haunted room. My wife was unaware of this in advance but said she had strange feelings about the room, which was No. 1. I took a photo and an orb was present at the exact spot she focused on. Now, I am very sceptical of orbs, which in the main part are undoubtedly explainable quirks of digital cameras, not, as many suggest, spirit energy. However, I must admit that it was slightly peculiar that it appeared at exactly the right spot.

White Hart,
Exeter, Devon

WHITE HART, PADSTOW, CORNWALL

Originally built as a coaching inn the White Hart occupies a Grade II listed sixteenth-century building. It has been carefully and completely restored and now offers the highest standard of comfortable accommodation, located in a wing of the main house.

A former landlady and landlord had a number of peculiar experiences here that they believed related to a former visitor, an asthmatic priest who had stayed here many years ago after failing to secure a bed at a local clerical resting place. Unfortunately, this priest had died later the same night from an asthma attack. Strange breathing noises have often been heard in the bedroom in which he died. The former occupants also said that hearing unexplained footsteps was commonplace and they usually sounded as if someone had passed the living room and was walking upstairs. On one occasion a person stood on the stairs actually heard the footsteps pass by them! Apparently their pet dog would also often become very anxious for no obvious reason, items such as milk bottles would move seemingly of their own accord and doors would open by themselves.

Many years ago two builders who were working on the property saw two ghostly figures in an upstairs room. They knew they were the only people there and that the building was locked so there could not have been any real person there.

William IV, Truro, Cornwall

The William IV is an excellent pub and has recently been refurbished, though the fact that is rectangular means that when it is busy it can get very congested. The pub has an excellent friendly atmosphere and the beer garden is great in the summer months. It has been stated that the pub was built on the site of a Dominican friary and it is indeed an ecclesiastical brother who allegedly haunts the pub.

William IV, Totnes, Devon

Locals best know this pub as the King Bill, and the inn certainly has a warm and friendly atmosphere. It is a welcoming, well-known pub in the heart of the picturesque town of Totnes, on the corner of Fore Street and Station Road. This rounded brick building replaced an earlier Elizabethan-style one demolished in 1902. Mrs Thomas Coombe ran the inn in 1901 and soon after an omnibus coach service to Paignton operated from the hotel (three times daily in summer months, and twice daily in winter months). The road junction by the hotel (Station Road) was built in 1830 to enable traffic coming from Bridgetown to get to Ashburton without having to pass through the rest of the upper town.

A cook named Bill who used to work here allegedly haunts this inn. He is described as an elderly gent and mostly appears in the upper rooms of the pub. Also, the building has previously been party to strange poltergeist activity such as electrical problems and objects moving without seemingly being touched. This has all been blamed on Old Bill (not the police I hasten to add).

William IV Hotel, Totnes, Devon

CHAPTER 22

Ye Olde Burtle Inn, Burtle, Somerset

Ye Olde Burtle Inn is a traditional Olde English pub and restaurant located in the small village of Burtle within the Somerset Levels. Originally a cider house, although now much larger, the inn has retained many original features from years ago. The pub also has its own cider, made from apples grown in the orchard behind it; it is probably the last pub in England to do this. Some original cob walling can still be seen and years ago a skittle alley was added. More recent additions include a patio and Taverna – a wonderful suntrap from midday onwards – and camping pitches in the orchard.

In February 2005, I accompanied a small team of six others for an all-night investigation. The team remained as one group for the majority of the night, but with individuals spread out over the rooms as and when necessary. A very interesting building with excellent hospitality, but it is always difficult to conduct an investigation in a working pub. However, thanks to the seriousness with which our host approached the situation, this was one of the best pub investigations we have attended. A relaxed and informal approach was promoted with the idea of making the investigation as easy-going as we could. We wanted to try and create a feeling of calm and normality, which features in the majority of reported ghost sightings and encounters. Initially, we confined ourselves to the upstairs level of the building, but we ventured downstairs after closing time. Because live in staff would be sleeping upstairs, the team then remained downstairs. Two of the team members dowsed separately in different rooms at different times, not discussing results to avoid cross-contamination. For simplicity's sake, the most interesting results are listed.

In the upstairs office a male presence named George, aged sixty-four and who died in the 1740s came to light. He had formerly lived here and died in the area. It appeared that he was not a particularly pleasant person and had been known as something of a philanderer. In an upstairs corridor there a female presence aged about two was located. She had died in 1822. In the skittle alley there was a male aged twenty-nine.

In the lounge the team identified an old man, aged eighty-three who had died as recently as 1974. His name was Eric Hiliopthorpe, a local man who always sat in the same place but said that the chair he was near wasn't the same chair (we later verified that the chair is new to the pub). He had sadly died of a heart attack on his way to or from the pub. There was also a girl called Francis, aged about seven and who'd died in 1694. She is happy and likes to run around downstairs and has apparently been seen by various visitors to the pub. The team also tracked a woman who walks up and down the bar and then down to the toilets. Here she pauses and then walks to the restaurant but pauses at the door and then heads back to the bar. This is Anna, aged twenty-four, who died in 1803. Unbeknown to any of us a washerwoman has been seen in this exact locations identified by the team.

In the main bar there was an area where almost everyone felt a tingly, static spot on several occasions. Some team members were convinced that this was because of the presence of a spirit, the dowsing rods often confirming that one was present. This was below the area in the centre of the corridor upstairs, where a similar feeling had also been picked up on. Feelings such as shudders or of something being there were also encountered in other areas downstairs, notably in the vicinity of the chair in front of the alcove with an iron gate in front of it. This is presumed to have been a door or stairway in the past and is the same spot where a dowser picked up the spirit of a man. At one point a small EMF fluctuation was also picked up in front of the same chair which had not been there beforehand.

One investigator heard and saw the door in the corridor leading from the serving area of the restaurant to the kitchens, swinging back and forth three times as if someone had just rushed through it. The restaurant and lounge were empty and another person was close enough to confirm this sighting. The rest of the team were in the bar area and confirmed that no one had passed though or been seen to go up the stairs, which had been heard to creak. Subsequent attempts to recreate this by looking for loose floorboards or pushing the door failed.

Séances were held in the bar, lounge and restaurant, but these produced little results that could not be explained by the live-in staff moving around upstairs or the thermal expansion and contraction of the heating system and building. However, laughter was heard in the bar and several cold spots were felt including a measured drop of around 5°c. The candle flickered often in time to a response to a question and tapping noises were also heard. Another person and myself both heard a yelping noise like when a dog is dreaming, coming from the lounge area. It was later revealed that the owner's dog had recently passed on, but there was no dog there at the time of our visit.

Then in May 2006 we ran an all-night ghost hunt to raise money for charity and had another interesting night, which included a trip to the sight of the Battle of Sedgemoor where we all heard strange tapping and metal clanking noises – dare I say that it sounded like the clash of swords. We investigated and there appeared to be no metal in the vicinity. The investigation at the inn was quiet although one guest felt very uneasy by the fireplace and nearly passed out. This is where the owner claims that a vicar died. Another guest had carried out an automatic writing experiment and had independently started writing the letters 'V, I, C'.

BIBLIOGRAPHY

Addicoat, I., *Ghosthunting: A Tour of West Cornwall's Ghosts*

Addicoat, I., *Ghostly tales of Cornwall*

Addicoat, I., *Haunted Devon*

Addicoat, I., *Haunted St Ives*

Addicoat, I., Buswell G., *Mysteries of the Cornish Coast*

Alexander, M., *A Companion to the Folklore, Myths & Customs of Britain*

Barber, S. and C., *Haunted Pubs in Devon*

Barber, S. and C., *Ghastly & Ghostly Devon*

Barber, S. and C., *Ghosts of Exeter*

Brown, T., *Ghosts of Devon*

Chard, J., *Haunted Happenings in Devon*

Green, A., *Haunted Inns & Taverns*

Hammond, N., *Ghosts of Plymouth*

Hippesley-Coxe, *A Haunted Britain*

Holgate, M., *Celebrity Ghosts of Devon*

Jones, R., *Haunted Britain & Ireland*

Jones, R., *Haunted Inns of Britain & Ireland*

Karl, J., *Great Ghost Hunt*

Lyon-Playfair, G., *Haunted Pub Guide*

Matthews, R., *Haunted Bath*

Mullins, R., *The Inn on the Moor: A History of Jamaica Inn*

Newman, R., *Haunted Cornwall*

Royal, M., Given, I., *Local Ghosts*

Underwood, P., *A Gazetteer of British Ghosts*

Underwood, P., *Ghosts of Cornwall*

Underwood, P., *Ghosts of Devon*

Underwood, P., *Ghosts of North Devon*

Underwood, P., *Ghosts of Somerset*

Underwood, P., *Guide to Ghosts & Haunted Places*

Underwood, P., *Westcountry Hauntings*

Vesey, B. – *Hidden Inns of the West Country*

Westwood, J. – *Gothick Cornwall*

Williams, M. – *Ghosthunting South West*

Williams, M. – *Ghosts of Bodmin Moor*

Williams, M. – *Psychic Phenomena*

Williams, M. – *Supernatural Adventure*